A Plea to Economists Who Favour Liberty: Assist the Everyman

A Plea to Economists Who Favour Liberty: Assist the Everyman

DANIEL B. KLEIN

WITH COMMENTARIES BY
JOHN FLEMMING
CHARLES GOODHART
ISRAEL M. KIRZNER
DEIRDRE MCCLOSKEY
GORDON TULLOCK

The Institute of Economic Affairs

First published in Great Britain in 2001 by
The Institute of Economic Affairs
2 Lord North Street
Westminster
London SW1P 3LB
in association with Profile Books Ltd

A CIP catalogue record for this book is available from the British Library.

ISBN 0 255 36501 2

Many IEA publications are translated into languages other than English or are reprinted. Permission to translate or to reprint should be sought from the General Director at the address above.

Typeset in Stone by MacGuru
info@macguru.org.uk

Printed and bound in Great Britain by Hobbs the Printers

CONTENTS

THE AUTHORS

Daniel B. Klein

Daniel Klein received his BS degree in economics from George Mason University, Fairfax, Virginia, and his PhD from New York University. He was Assistant Professor at University of California, Irvine, and since 1996 has been Associate Professor at Santa Clara University. At SCU, he is also the General Director of the Civil Society Institute (www.scu.edu/csi). He is a member of the IEA Academic Advisory Council.

He has published scholarly research in a number of areas: urban transit, modern toll roads, auto emissions, private toll roads of nineteenth-century America, credit reporting, FDA drug approval, quality and safety assurance by voluntary means, the discovery factors of economic freedom, the distinction between Schelling co-ordination and Hayek co-ordination, and how government officials come to believe in the goodness of bad policy.

He is co-author of *Curb Rights: A Foundation for Free Enterprise in Urban Transit* (Brookings Institution, 1997); editor of *Reputation: Studies in the Voluntary Elicitation of Good Conduct* (University of Michigan Press, 1997); author of *Assurance and Trust in a Great Society* (Foundation for Economic Education, 2000); and he has published articles in many scholarly journals. His work has won the Sir Antony Fisher Award for Best Public Policy Book, the

Smith Prize in Austrian Economics, the Hayek Essay Prize from the Mont Pèlerin Society, and the Ehrlich Prize for Best Economics Dissertation (NYU).

His articles on the economics profession have been published in *Challenge*, *Ideas on Liberty*, *USA Today* magazine and *Wirtschafts Politische Blaetter*. He edited *What Do Economists Contribute?* (Macmillan, 1999; Palgrave paperback ed., 2001), a collection of nine essays by great twentieth-century classical-liberal economists.

John Flemming FBA

John Flemming, Warden of Wadham College, Oxford, since October 1993, was Chief Economist of the European Bank for Reconstruction and Development from March 1991 to December 1993, working on the problems of the transition economies of eastern Europe. Previously he had been an Executive Director of the Bank of England which he joined as Chief Economic Adviser in 1980. He had spent the previous twenty years in Oxford, as a student, and then from 1965 to 1980 as an Official Fellow in Economics at Nuffield College, where he taught macro-economics, public finance, capital theory, etc. He was involved in editing *Oxford Economic Papers*, the *Review of Economic Studies* and the *Economic Journal*, and has published articles in several academic economic journals as well as a book on inflation, and chapters contributed to other collections. He is a Vice-President of the Royal Economic Society, Treasurer of the British Academy and a member of the Royal Commission on Environmental Pollution. He chaired an inquiry into the regulatory regime for privatised public utilities in the UK, and has chaired the National Institute of Economic and Social Research since 1997.

Charles Goodhart CBE, FBA

Charles Goodhart is the Norman Sosnow Professor of Banking and Finance at the London School of Economics. Before joining the LSE in 1985, he worked at the Bank of England for seventeen years as a monetary adviser, becoming a Chief Adviser in 1980. In 1997 he was appointed one of the outside independent members of the Bank of England's new Monetary Policy Committee until May 2000. Earlier he taught at Cambridge and LSE. Besides numerous articles, he has written two books on monetary history, and a graduate monetary textbook, *Money, Information and Uncertainty* (second ed. 1989); has published two collections of papers on monetary policy, *Monetary Theory and Practice* (1984) and *The Central Bank and the Financial System* (1995); and an institutional study of *The Evolution of Central Banks,* revised and republished (MIT Press) in 1988.

Israel M. Kirzner

Israel Kirzner received his bachelor's degree at Brooklyn College, Brooklyn, NY, and his master's and doctoral degrees at New York University (where he studied under the late Ludwig von Mises). Since 1957 he has been a faculty member at New York University, holding the title of Professor of Economics since 1968. Professor Kirzner's published works include *The Economic Point of View* (1960); *Competition and Entrepreneurship* (1973); *Discovery and the Capitalist Process* (1985); *The Meaning of Market Process* (1992); *How Markets Work: Disequilibrium, Entrepreneurship and Discovery* (1997); *The Driving Force of the Market, Essays in Austrian Economics* (2000); and 'Entrepreneurial Discovery and the Competitive Market Process: An Austrian Approach', in the *Journal of Economic*

Literature, March 1997. For the IEA he contributed a paper, 'The Primacy of Entrepreneurial Discovery', to *The Prime Mover of Progress*, IEA Readings No. 23 (1980).

Deirdre McCloskey

Deirdre McCloskey teaches economics, history, English and philosophy at the University of Illinois at Chicago, where she is UIC Distinguished Professor, and at Erasmusuniversteit Rotterdam, where she is Tinbergen Professor. For twelve years she was on the faculty of economics at the University of Chicago. Author of twelve books and two hundred scholarly articles, her most recent books are *How to Be Human Though an Economist* and *Measurement and Meaning in Economics: The Essential Deirdre McCloskey*, edited by S. Ziliak. Her memoir, *Crossing*, was a *New York Times* Notable Book of 1999. She is currently working on linguistic economics, formalism in science, and ethics in a commercial society.

Gordon Tullock

Gordon Tullock was born in 1922 in Illinois. He attended the University of Chicago, where he took a law course with time out for military service. While in law school he took one course in economics from Henry Simons. As a result he became a lifelong student of economics, although he is largely self-taught. After a period of time as a China expert for the Department of State he became an academic economist, and has held appointments in a number of American universities, of which the most significant are the University of Virginia, the Virginia Polytechnic Institute and George Mason University, where he is now. He has published widely, mainly in the fields of economics and public choice. Recently he has been working in evolutionary biology, and is President of the International Bieconomics Society. His books include *The Calculus of Consent*, co-authored with James Buchanan, *The Politics of Bureaucracy*, *The Social Dilemma*, *The Economics of Non-Human Societies*, and many others. He founded the journal *Public Choice* and for 25 years edited it. He is a past president of the Public Choice Society, the Western Economic Association, the Southern Economic Association, and the Atlantic Economic Society.

FOREWORD

There is a long-standing dispute in the economics profession about the extent to which economists should indulge in policy prescriptions. Should they remain detached scholars, pursuing their research to the satisfaction of themselves and their fellow academics? Or should they try to educate their fellow men and women in economic ideas, generating and interpreting information which will be relevant to policies pursued by governments or other organisations?

In Occasional Paper 118, Professor Daniel Klein of Santa Clara University contrasts the 'scholasticism' of some famous twentieth-century economists, such as George Stigler, with the 'public discourse' school, which can be identified at least as far back as the writings of Adam Smith. Writing for economists in the 'more libertarian half of the economics profession', Klein argues that Stigler was wrong to dismiss the idea of 'the economist as preacher', and possibly also wrong in his belief that economists have an almost imperceptible influence on society.

To become more influential and to improve the quality of decision-making, particularly by government, economists should learn how to appeal to the 'Everyman'. They should, says Klein, make 'sensible and informed use of basic economic insights and low-tech forms of evidence'. High standards of research depend on a degree of scholasticism, but it is too much emphasised.

Scholastic norms should be relaxed to encourage teaching and research which are relevant to policy. Benefits would include a reduction in the power of rent-seekers.

Five well-known economists then comment on Professor Klein's paper. John Flemming, Warden of Wadham College, Oxford, points to the varying incentives which induce economists to concentrate on different forms of output, including the 'pernicious' influence in Britain of the Research Assessment Exercise for universities.

Professor Charles Goodhart, of the London School of Economics, argues that Klein exaggerates his case. He sees no shortage of economists engaged in public debate in Europe, and doubts whether there is such a deficiency in the United States either. Liberal economists, in particular, have 'done rather well in the battle for the public ear in recent decades'.

Professor Israel Kirzner, of New York University, is generally sympathetic to Klein's views but believes that he goes too far in urging economists to try to change the values of the public. The economist should teach people what policies will promote their welfare as they see it: going beyond that risks the loss of the economist's reputation for 'scrupulous disinterestedness'.

According to Professor Deirdre McCloskey, of the University of Illinois at Chicago, Klein is too kind about the scientific achievements of mainstream economics: she doubts whether 'anything much of value scientifically has come out of American academic economics since . . . 1950'. She would go farther than Klein in getting back to Adam Smith and encouraging policy-relevant science.

In the final commentary, before a response from Professor Klein, Professor Gordon Tullock, of George Mason University, disagrees with Klein on one point. In his view, in contrast to Klein's, 'an ambitious young economist' will not just benefit the world but will find it in his or her own career interests to make some efforts to improve policy by 'publishing or speaking to a non-economic audience'.

As in all Institute publications, the views expressed in this Occasional Paper are those of the authors, not those of the Institute (which has no corporate view), its Managing Trustees, Academic Advisory Council members or senior staff. The Paper is published as a stimulus to debate on the extent to which economists should be involved in influencing public policy.

COLIN ROBINSON

Editorial Director, Institute of Economic Affairs
Professor of Economics, University of Surrey

ACKNOWLEDGEMENTS

The author thanks the Social Philosophy and Policy Center, at Bowling Green (Ohio) State University, for affording time and very agreeable conditions to rethink and revise this paper during the fall of 1998.

SUMMARY

- Some libertarian economists put personal faith in an invisible hand, believing that if they do well academically they will do good for society at large.

- But economists do well academically mainly by producing technical *curiosa*. This work is rarely important to policy issues and authentic argumentation.

- Society would gain much from wise policy reform. Yet policy is made, not by trained economists, but by every public official and ordinary voter. The 'Everyman' is the true practitioner of political economy.

- The insights wanting in the Everyman's economic understanding are *certain basic ideas*. To the professional economist who understands these basics, they may seem too pedestrian to bother with.

- Nincompoop libertarian economists neglect the Everyman because there is no academic payoff to teaching him the basics.

- Many academic economists disdain policy argumentation and outspokenness because they wish to sublimate the practitioner predicament of their discipline. An economist might damage his academic career by communicating with the Everyman.

- Many great classical-liberal economists have faced up to the practitioner predicament. They have tried to cultivate the reward of esteem for economists who do good.
- Libertarian economists need to work out their own professional conflicts and existential confusions. Coming to a more Smithian understanding of the character of their discipline, they would be better able to stand together, when appropriate, against their establishment-minded colleagues, and give economics an authority it is now lacking.

FIGURES

A Plea to Economists Who Favour Liberty: Assist the Everyman

1 INTRODUCTION

Adam Smith (1776) wrote of political economy 'as a branch of the science of the statesman or legislator' (p. 397). *The Wealth of Nations* has long been described as 'a tract for the times, a specific attack on certain types of government activity' (Viner, 1927: 218). Smith underscored the moral purpose of his work: 'the cheapness of consumption and the encouragement given to production . . . [are] precisely the two effects which it is *the great business of political economy to promote*' (p. 706, italics added).

Smith noted that people often have a poor understanding of public affairs. Landowners are 'too often defective' in having a 'tolerable knowledge' of how their interest relates to society's (p. 249). The labourer, too, 'is incapable either of comprehending [society's interest], or of understanding its connexion with his own' (p. 249). Regarding the buying and hold of wheat, '[t]he popular fear of engrossing and forestalling may be compared to the popular terrors and suspicions of witchcraft' (p. 500). Although Smith often attributed bad policy to shrewd political manipulations, he also saw bad policy flowing from ignorance and foolish prejudices. He hoped folly would be lessened by the efforts of political economists.

The Nobel laureate economist George Stigler (1982) says Smith was wrong: 'there is little reason to accept Smith's implicit assumption that the main source of error is ignorance or "prejudice"' (p. 143). Stigler faults Adam Smith for preaching:

> Smith gave a larger role to emotion, prejudice, and
> ignorance in political life than he ever allowed in ordinary
> economic affairs. . . . Smith's attitude toward political
> behavior was not dissimilar to that of a parent toward a
> child: the child was often mistaken and sometimes perverse,
> but normally it would improve in conduct if properly
> instructed . . . Therefore reforms must be effected, if effected
> they can be, by moral suasion. (pp. 140, 142–3)

Stigler argues against 'the economist as preacher'. In the political process, people pursue their self-interest, and rarely can the economist make the citizen better informed of her own interests. People choose and search and think optimally: 'we deal with people who maximize their utility, and it would be both inconsistent and idle for us to urge people not to do so' (p. 6). Stigler is, however, willing to pardon Adam Smith for doing so: 'it would be anachronistic to lament Smith's failure to discuss the problem of the optimum investment of the individual in the acquisition of knowledge' (p. 145) – that is, the problem discussed in Stigler (1961).

Adam Smith, by contrast, believed that public discourse could produce genuine learning and persuasion, and that economists should participate. Public discourse is not mere charade contrived to pass the time. Speakers claim to value the public interest and to some extent make sacrifices to live up to that claim. The public interest is complex and controversial, but through the instruction and moral force of conversation people can be persuaded to think and act differently. Even if this is true only in rare instances, those are the instances that matter most.

Stigler would have us believe that the persuasive power of conversation is negligible. The incentives of citizens to obtain relevant knowledge are unaffected by anything the economist has to say. They know their interest and respond optimally to the cost of acquiring information: 'Every failure of a person to make decisions which serve his self-interest may be interpreted as an error in logic' (Stigler, 1982: 144). Short of helping people with their logic, which they have strong incentives to get right, conversation is otiose. Because Stigler insists on reducing knowledge to information and logic, he insists on eradicating other facets of knowledge. So great was his insistence, he took to finding and correcting all the errors and inconsistencies of the passages in *The Wealth of Nations* regarding the political process (Stigler, 1982, chap. 12).

But perhaps Smith had it right after all. There is more to knowledge than information and logic: there is also interpretation and judgement. Stigler's famous papers (1961, 1962) cannot deal with interpretation and judgement. Stigler worked hard to eradicate from economics the subtler facets of knowledge. He wanted to believe that his papers on information had captured the essence of knowledge. Hence he developed a blindness to facets of knowledge that might make a rival claim to the essence of knowledge. Cases in point are Stigler's animosities, continued today by Stiglerian economists, against Austrian economics and Deirdre McCloskey.

Public discourse shapes and influences the political process. From the political process emerge policy decisions. Rent-seekers lobby for measures that injure the public interest. (Lobbyists on the good side of issues are not considered rent-seekers.) Rent-seekers decide what quantity of resources to devote to rent-seeking. Economists can stymie rent-seeking by taking part in public discourse and the political process. Economists can use their power of persuasion to reduce the expected benefits of rent-seeking.

Thus policy is explained partly by the behaviour of economists. But what explains the behaviour of economists? Partly, the professional rewards and punishments for taking part in public discourse, or the character of the economics profession. Good policy depends on economic enlightenment, which depends on the participation of economists, which depends on the incentives for economists, which depend on the practices and standards of the economics profession. Government policy would be better if the economists who favour liberty thought more seriously about how they contribute to society.

My implied reader is an economist who belongs to the more libertarian half of the economics profession. Readers who are not economists might find parallels with their own professional fields.

2 A MISPLACED FAITH IN AN INVISIBLE HAND

Stigler (1982) told us that 'economists exert a minor and scarcely detectable influence on the societies in which they live' (p. 63). He suggests, for example, that economists' testimony in antitrust cases has had small influence. 'Knowledgeable economists have proposed much more favorable verdicts on our influence,' he says, 'but they do not offer evidence of a specificity or power such as we normally require in professional work' (p. 48).

Perhaps Stigler is correct about the small influence of economists. But whatever the magnitude, the pertinent question is: Do economists better aid society by participating in public discourse or by concentrating on scholastic work? Stigler favours scholastic work:

Please do not read into my low valuation of the importance of professional preaching a similarly low valuation of scientific work. Once a general relationship in economic phenomena is discovered and verified, it becomes a part of the working knowledge of everyone. A newly established scientific relationship shifts the arena of discourse and is fully adopted by all informed parties, whatever their policy stands. Whether a person likes the price system or dislikes it and prefers a form of non-price rationing of some good, he must accept the fact of a negatively sloping demand curve and take account of its workings. The most influential economist, even in the area of public policy, is the

economist who makes the most important scientific
contributions. (Stigler, 1982: 34; see also p. 67 and Stigler,
1988: 85, 179).

Yet in his favourable verdict on the influence of 'important scientific contributions', Stigler does not offer evidence of a specificity or power such as we normally require in professional work.
In fact, his pronouncements are practically vacuous. He supposes
that professional economists, even when publishing in scholastic
journals, establish definitive verification of economic truths. An
'established scientific relationship . . . is fully adopted by all informed parties'. Stigler provides no grounds for believing that
'informed parties' are sufficiently great to effect the policy im-
provements for which 'established scientific relationships' ostensi-
bly pave the way. And what does Stigler have in mind when he
speaks of 'an established scientific relationship'? Is it an established scientific relationship that free, private enterprise is better
at serving society than government enterprise, or that minimum
wage laws hurt the poor, or that occupational licensing hurts the
poor? If so, have these become 'a part of the working knowledge of
everyone'? In America, government remains as interventionist as
ever.

Stigler refers to 'newly established scientific relationships' as
though working scientists generate such things at a steady pace.
Yet the one example he gives of an established scientific relationship is hundreds of years old: when the price of a good goes up,
people buy less of it. Stigler refrains from naming an 'established
scientific relationship' produced by economists during his life-
time.

Stigler argues his point by referring to 'the most influential economist'. But ordinary researchers, even at the 'top' departments, will never make major contributions like the law of demand. How are *we* to earn our self-respect? Stigler (1982) preached that our comparative advantage is in scholasticism, not public discourse: 'it is the judgment of the science that is decisive in judging a scholar's achievements' (p. 147). He urged us to pursue research expressed to other academics in terms of the official paradigms. He affirmed a faith in *scholasticism* (and 1980s *JPE*-style Chicagoism in particular).

Stigler and Sherwin Rosen (1997: 151) say doing well academically is doing good for society – an invisible-hand result. One wonders, does it apply to sociology, anthropology and women's studies? After all, those academic 'industries' have essentially the same institutional structure as economics. Also, why do these free marketeers put such faith in an 'industry' that is predominantly government employed? (See Roey et al., 1999: 8 on public versus private college and university faculty employment.)

3 HAYEK AND OTHERS DOUBT THAT DOING WELL IS DOING GOOD

Other economists view economics differently, and have little faith in an invisible hand. Friedrich Hayek (1944) noted that 'those who have to apply economic theory are laymen, not really trained as economists. [Economists] can at most be called in as advisors while the actual decisions must be left to the statesman and the general public' (p. 37). Whereas Stigler puts his faith in the profession – where economists talk to economists – the Smithian attitude recognises that *the true practitioner of political economy is every public official and ordinary voter*. To contribute to human betterment, economists need to reach the Everyman.

As Ronald Coase (1975) notes: 'what [economists] have to say which is important and true is quite simple . . . . What is discouraging is that it is these simple truths which are so commonly ignored in the discussion of economic policy' (p. 49). Cutting-edge academic research is not of value even to one who sits at the right hand of presidents. Martin Anderson claims that not once in his four-year experience as a Reagan administration economist, 'in countless meetings on national economic policy, did anyone ever refer to any article from an academic journal. Not once did anyone use a mathematical formula more complicated than adding, subtracting, multiplying, or dividing' (Anderson, 1992: 95). Lawrence Summers (1991: 146), Herbert Stein (quoted in Hamilton, 1992: 62), Ronald Coase (1975: 59-60) and other prominent economists have stressed that the theory and evidence with real *oomph* are very low tech. Millions of Americans have been persuaded by economic arguments that drug policy should move towards legalisation and schooling should be choice-driven. None of those arguments relies much on fancy models or statistical significance.

Coase quotes Frank Knight, who said the following in a presidential address to the American Economic Association in 1950:

> I have been increasingly moved to wonder whether my job is
> a job or a racket, whether economists, and particularly
> economic theorists, may not be in a position that Cicero,
> concerning Cato, ascribed to the augurs of Rome – that they
> should cover their faces or burst into laughter when they
> met on the street . . . (Knight, 1951: 2, quoted in Coase, 1975:
> 54).

Knight also says that it is basics which are needed in public discourse, not scholastic crafts: 'The serious fact is that the bulk of the really important things that economics has to teach are things that people would see for themselves if they were willing to see.' The important role for economists is to make people *willing to see* certain basics.

Stigler (1967) eradicates the subtleties of the will, of thought and of discourse: 'In neoclassical economics, the producer is always at a production frontier' (p. 215). And that goes also for the producer of beliefs, arguments and policy decisions. The frontier is made up of information and logic, neither of which depends on the economist. Compare Stigler's fatalistic view with that of Thomas Schelling, in an address to young economists:

> There are not just free lunches but banquets awaiting the
> former socialist countries that can institute enforceable
> contract, copyrights, and patents, or eliminate rent-free

housing and energy subsidies . . . [I]t is economists who help to find where we are deep inside [the] frontier, diagnose what keeps us from the frontier, and propose institutional changes to bring us closer to the frontier. To those of you who become professional economists I urge you: get out there and help find those free lunches. (Schelling, 1995: 22)

4 AN IMPOVERISHED UNDERSTANDING OF KNOWLEDGE

Stigler's view that we economists should always draw the individual's frontiers so that he is at the frontier (never deep inside it) is an extension of his framework for decision-making in general: the exclusion of the very notion of error (see Stigler, 1976). In particular, Stigler would reject Israel Kirzner's theory of error, which is the theoretical inverse of Kirzner's theory of entrepreneurship. Kirzner teaches that breakthroughs in knowledge sometimes come from interpretive *insight*, not mere information. Some interpretive insights are adequately described neither as the result of deliberate search nor the result of sheer chance. Kirzner (1985) wants us to recognize a third, entrepreneurial, kind of discovery, from a human source that is 'undeliberate but motivated' (p. 14). To admit of entrepreneurial discovery in their thinking, economists must recognise that knowledge is not merely information but also interpretation. Stigler and his followers have often disparaged Kirzner's work, because they cannot admit of the interpretive element of knowledge (see Klein, 1999a).

If exceptional interpretive insight may be called entrepreneurial discovery, the neglect of interpretive insights that are obvious may be called error. Kirzner (1983) reviewed Stigler's book *The Economist as Preacher and Other Essays* and emphasised that Stigler's denial of error is the root of his vision for economists: 'It is Stigler's perverse consistency in this regard that has led him to his odd conclusions regarding the possibility of valuable economic policy advice' (p. 40). Kirzner's pupil Sanford Ikeda (1997a, 1997b) has usefully distinguished two interpretations of bad policy: the *deception thesis*, in which posturing politicians and rent-seekers laugh all the way to the bank, and the *error thesis*, in which decent and good-willed human beings blunder inexpertly through the complex realms of political economy and trap themselves in a cul-de-sac. Stigler says, essentially, that all bad policy arises through deception or knavery, and education through public discourse is not worth the effort. Ikeda maintains, like Smith, Hayek and Coase, that much bad policy comes from intellectual error, not knavery. Kirzner agrees and says that Stigler's position is a lamentable error: 'It will be unfortunate indeed if [Stigler's] fascinating volume succeeds in popularizing the altogether unfounded notion that greater and more widespread economic understanding can make no contribution to the betterment of the human condition' (p. 40).[1]

That knowledge is not merely information was known to Adam Smith. Smith said that the ordinary labourer lacked not just information but understanding in judging how his interest relates to the interest of society: 'his education and habits are commonly such as to render him unfit to *judge* even though he was *fully informed*' (Smith, 1776: 249, italics added). Stigler's attempts to flatten knowledge down to information led him not only to a blindness to interpretation; it led also to a blindness to *judgement*. When interpretations are multiple the individual has to decide which interpretation to take stock in. Judgement is the belief facet

---

1   In his earlier years, Stigler seems to have been more willing to hold a theoretical place for the idea of error; see Stigler, 1958: 74.

of knowledge, and it is revealed by action. In belief, as Michael Polanyi (1962) explained, there is an element of commitment. One's beliefs partly determine what one does. Judgement is the moral dimension of knowledge, affecting what it is that one will stand for. It is stressed in the work of Deirdre McCloskey (1994: 375).

Economists tend to think of interests as given and fixed. But economists can provide guidance about *what their listeners' interests should be*. Man has hierarchical values and hierarchical decision-making powers. We cannot deny that, while each level may be seen to be optimising, the next level knows that there may exist yet-undiscovered superior alternative interpretations of the information possessed, so that judgement remains perennially open to revision. Hence the individual always has the potential to transcend whatever framework (including preferences) he consciously recognises or explicitly models for himself (Hayek, 1952: 193–4). Humans are in a constant process of discovering and remaking their deeper preferences. Therefore it makes sense to speak of some deeper level of self that chooses, or at least influences, our interests. This influence from deeper levels depends on how the deeper levels are prompted and on how one is equipped to respond to signals from deeper levels. For judgement on economic matters, economists can be the source of deeper insights and can prompt deeper values, having an influence like that which a parent has on a child.

Students of rhetoric from Smith (1762: 63) to McCloskey (1985: 121) stress that persuasive authority flows from the character or *ethos* of the speaker. Smith says that Jonathan Swift compellingly assumes the character of a plain man, and that in doing so he persuades by simply stating, 'I have always been of opinion that . . .'

(p. 38). When an economist argues against licensing restrictions, the argument persuades because of its logical cogency and factual support, but also because it comes from a sincere, scrupulous and capable economist. Even without fact or logic, the economist's opinion carries weight. If a listener receives an economist supposedly in good faith and then utterly disregards the economist's opinion, he behaves like a cad. To believe that *ethos* cuts no ice with listeners is to believe that every listener is a cad. Those who do not believe that every listener is a cad will agree that the economist's opinion can influence the listener's decision as to what to believe.

McCloskey has suggested that the economics profession as a whole is like the drunk who looks for his lost keys under the lamppost because the light is better there. I wish to revise the parable. The public official and ordinary voter – the Everyman – is searching for the lost keys, and the economist *knows very well where they are*. The location of the 'keys' is one matter of concurrence between Smith and Stigler (and the rather libertarian implied reader of this essay).

In the body politic, the economist ought to be a moral agent who identifies policy error, reproaches those who commit such errors, and educates for the avoidance and correction of error. Yet many economists do no such things. Instead they take up Stigler's attitude, and confine themselves to the small area of rarefied light under their profession's lamppost.[2] The Everyman often fails to

2   In my reading of Stigler, he underwent an attitudinal change during the late 1970s and 1980s, becoming more parochial in thought, imperious in paradigm, and fatalistic in politics. It is with significant misgivings that I decry a man who was president of the Mont Pèlerin Society (1976–78) and who, as Machovec (1995: 209) puts it, 'truly deserves to be known as John the Baptist of the new learning' in industrial organisation.

Figure 1   **Unless economists participate, rent-seekers will invest in access A_1 to influence policymakers**

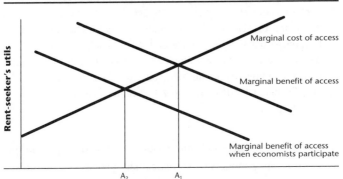

Rent-seeker's access to policymakers

find the keys simply because the economist disdains to show him where they are.

Were the economist to take a greater role in public discourse, rent-seeking would be better foiled. By providing facts, logics, interpretations and moral authority the economist can influence voters and policymakers. The economist can even influence rent-seekers, who also feel some responsibility to side with the public interest, as they understand it.

Figure 1 shows a calculus of rent-seeking. The horizontal axis measures access to policymakers. The marginal cost of access is increasing. Access to policymakers brings the chance of favourable (but antisocial) policy. The rent-seeker's optimal level of access is A_1, where marginal benefit equals marginal cost. But economists might feel an incentive or responsibility to step forward. They address policymakers or the public and persuade them not to be too accommodating. Coase (1975) speaks of this role of economists:

> At any rate, it may be that there is room for economists'
> views on public policy to play a valuable part in the process
> of modification and change, even though they will usually
> not be able to exercise a decisive influence over the choice of
> the policy itself. Certainly, however ill-advised policies may
> be, they are not in their administration devoid of sense. The
> demand for nonsense seems to be subject to the universal
> law of demand: we demand less of it when the price is
> higher. (p. 55)

By virtue of basic economic reasoning applied adeptly to the issue – not fancy models or statistical significance – economists shift marginal benefit to the lower line in Figure 1. Now the rent-seeker opts for A_2 access. Another path of influence might be for the economists to persuade policymakers to raise the cost of access. Or they might address the rent-seekers themselves, and shame them into good sportsmanship and free competition.

As Smith (1790) said, 'When [a man of public spirit] cannot establish the right, he will not disdain to ameliorate the wrong' (p. 233). Coase puts it this way: 'An economist who, by his effort, is able to postpone by a week a government program which wastes $100 million a year (what I would consider a modest success) has, by his action, earned his salary for the whole of his life.' If economists can scuttle such programmes altogether, 'we will confer a great benefit on mankind – and be grossly underpaid' (pp. 57–8).

5 TULLOCK ON DOING GOOD

Gordon Tullock once gave an address entitled 'How to Do Well While Doing Good!' to a group of young economists at Virginia Polytechnic Institute. (The lecture remained unpublished for more than a decade.) Tullock also projects a Smithian voice, a voice strikingly different from George Stigler's. He begins by noting instances in which economists have made a difference, such as the reduction of tariffs and the abolition of the Civil Aeronautics Board. He proposes that young economists 'select some blatantly undesirable activity, preferably of a state or local government, and become a modest expert on it'.

> After becoming an expert, the economist should attempt to get media publicity. . . . The League of Women Voters, for example, tends to go about looking for good causes and you may be able to improve their taste. There are also various business groups, Rotary Clubs, and so on that are always on the lookout for a lecturer and that would give you an opportunity to provide some influence . . . Most economists only occasionally give lectures to something like the Rotary Club. I am suggesting that this aspect of professional life be sharply increased. . . . Even if there were no beneficial impact on your career, nevertheless, I would urge it on you . . . It is likely that you will do more good for the world by concentrating on abolishing some [undesirable government] organization in your locality than the average person does – indeed, very much more. (Tullock, 1984: 239)

Tullock creates incentives for economists to engage in such activities: to do so will permit the economist to know that he would have Tullock's esteem.

But Tullock's main appeal is to career interest. 'The average economist can benefit his career while simultaneously making a contribution to the public welfare' (p. 229). Tullock says that basic public policy research 'does have some potential for publication in the regular economic literature. *The Journal of Law and Economics, The Journal of Political Economy, Public Policy,* and others all are interested in such articles.' At a lower notch, but still professionally valuable, are publications with public policy think-tanks – 'I, as a matter of fact, have three such things on my own vitae.' Tullock even encourages 'articles in local newspapers, letters to the editor', and offers the following optimistic remark: 'I would imagine that in cost/benefit terms these things are considerably more highly paying than JPE articles because although the payoff is not as high, the cost of producing them is also low' (p. 237).

Tullock wants economists to take part in public discourse, to stymie rent-seeking by shifting the curves in Figure 1. He argues that such activities are both virtuous and profitable. In a career-interest calculus of the economist's participation in public discourse, Tullock argues that the optimal level is positive.

His statements were made in the early 1970s. Maybe things were different then, or maybe Tullock was disguising the facts to serve the greater good. In the economics profession today, excellent basic public policy work cannot get published in leading journals, or even secondary journals. And the academic-career payoff to think-tank work and general-interest articles is, on average, probably not above zero. Such work can count negatively. It reveals that one is 'unfocused', 'not a scientist', 'not a serious econo-

Figure 2 **Three positions on whether public discourse coincides with doing well and doing good**

Is it worthwhile for the libertarian economist to orient himself towards public discourse . . .

	from an academic-career point of view? (doing well)	from a general-interest (Smithian) point of view? (doing good)
YES	Tullock	Tullock Klein
NO	Stigler Klein	Stigler

mist', or, as establishment Democrats such as Solow (1999) and Krugman (2000) are quick to say, an 'ideologue'. Tullock's expression of personal esteem is noble, but the career advice is dubious. When a young libertarian economist with publications in policy work or non-academic periodicals asks my advice, I tell him to remove such items from his academic vitae. Especially at the more prestigious departments, the optimal participation in public discourse (from a narrow career-interest perspective) is close to zero.

Tullock says that you do well by doing good. Stigler says that you do good by doing well. I disagree with both. Figure 2 distinguishes the three positions as regards whether orienting oneself towards public discourse coincides with doing well and doing good.

6 DO ECONOMISTS BELIEVE IN WHAT THEY ARE DOING?

Most economists know not to take part in public discourse, and don't. The sad state of higher education in America has been the subject of many recent books. Many commentators conclude that the social sciences are solipsistic, overly specialised and formalistic, and operating with little consequence to the real world.

This criticism has been levelled against the economics profession in particular (Cassidy, 1996; *Economist*, 1997). Dissatisfied students in France have launched a movement for 'post-autistic economics', which has galvanised students well beyond France (see the websites at www.paecon.net). The profession has indeed suffered this criticism from many of its own, and from diverse ideological quarters. Many living economists have published unmistakably critical comments about the profession being overly specialised, formalistic or irrelevant.

The perennial nature, at least since the rise of the modern university, of the irrelevance problem in economics is evidenced by early criticism of the profession by Edwin Cannan (1933), W. H. Hutt (1936; see especially pp. 34–7, 207–17), Barbara Wootton (1938), Frank Graham (1942: xv–xx), Hayek (1944) and Knight (1951). Many of these authors stress that the practitioner of political economy is the Everyman.

Making economics more relevant would inevitably mean increasing the extent to which the economist expresses judgements on public issues. In contrast, Stigler preached against policy pronouncements. 'Most of us are more impatient to do good, and probably we are not sanguine about our ability to engage usefully in full time scientific work' (Stigler, 1982: 66–7). Political tracts like *The Road to Serfdom* and *Capitalism and Freedom* were written, then, because their authors doubted their ability to do economics. My suspicion, rather, is that Stigler denigrated the role of the economist-cum-public intellectual in part because he doubted his own ability to appeal to the Everyman and to exercise judgement responsibly.

Besides the several dozen vocal insiders, serious doubts quietly exist among insiders aplenty. Many economists harbour reservations about the emphasis placed on equilibrium model-building and statistical significance. The leery economist does not express her doubts publicly, because doing so might give her colleagues the idea that she does not like and admire what they – and even she herself – are doing. But economists do not really support the profession's norms as much as it may appear. Many economists feel locked into an undesirable co-ordination equilibrium in which they publicly falsify what they really think.

Arjo Klamer and David Colander conducted extensive interviews with graduate students at six top economics departments. They report:

> [T]he interviews suggested a definite tension, frustration, and cynicism that, in our view, went beyond the normal graduate school blues. There was a strong sense that economics was a game and that hard work in devising relevant models that demonstrated a deep understanding of institutions would have a lower payoff than devising models that were analytically neat; the facade, not the depth of knowledge, was important. This cynicism is not limited to

the graduate school experience, but is applied also to the state of the art as they perceive it. (Klamer and Colander, 1990: 18)

A fourth-year graduate student remarks:

We go to the money workshop. . . . All of us go, week after week, and come back and just laugh at their big reputations. What they do is usually very complicated and very implausible. (quoted in Klamer and Colander, 1990: 18)

Deirdre McCloskey argues that model-building (what she here refers to as A-Priming) has become deranged, and adds:

Everyone knows this, though they are less willing to say it about their own sub-field of economics than someone else's. Macroeconomists disdain the pointless A-Priming of the field of industrial organization. Game theorists in industrial organization disdain the pointless iteration of 2-by-2-by-2 models in trade theory. Trade theorists scorn the five-year cycle of theoretical fashion in macroeconomics. The situation has reached the same result as statistical significance: nobody believes the so-called 'science' of the other scientists. (McCloskey, 1996: 94)

Similarly, Thomas Mayer writes:

Most of the abstract theorists seem happy with the way economics is going. But many, perhaps the majority of economists, are not. Some continue playing the game because they believe that it is the only game in town, that there is no other way of doing research. Others play it cynically because following certain procedures, such as 'sticking in the maths,' is necessary to publish in good

journals, and thus to earn tenure. Probably quite a number
of the already tenured have responded by, more or less,
giving up on research. Certainly not to all, perhaps not even
to most, but to many economists, the rules and conventions
that currently determine what is considered good research
have become a hollow ideology. (Mayer, 1993: 3–4)

Lawrence Summers has written a hard-hitting indictment of econometric work, and also suggests that the practices that prevail are hollow:

All too often researchers, referees and editors fail to ask
these scientific questions. Instead, they ask the same
questions that jugglers' audiences ask – Have virtuosity and
skill been demonstrated? Was something difficult done?
Often these questions can be answered favorably even where
no substantive contribution is being made. (Summers, 1991:
146)

On the aeroplane returning home from the annual meeting of the American Economics Association, I asked the adjacent passenger, an economist also returning home, to explain the paper he had presented at the meeting. He proceeded to lay out a simple and ingenious numerical example. Within five minutes I understood the idea and admired him for it. I asked him what the rest of the paper was about. He answered that it was devoted to developing a formal model based on the core idea. I asked him if he thought the formal model really added anything beyond what was achieved by the numerical example. He candidly said no, with a friendly smile that said, 'We both know how this profession works.'

7 PUBLIC DISCOURSE VERSUS SCHOLASTICISM

In his book *Truth versus Precision in Economics*, Thomas Mayer (1993) argues that 'there is a trade-off between rigour and relevance' (p. 7). Mayer says that a theory of certain features of the American economy, or a theory of how public policy that affects certain economic activities should be reformed, consists of numerous links. Each link is an argument or piece of evidence. The worthiness (or truth) of the theory is the strength of the entire chain of arguments. In Mayer's view economists have not paid attention to the entire chain. The profession has instead revelled in 'the principle of the strongest link' (Mayer, 1993: 57; see also Boettke, 1997). Economists have refined, strengthened and polished the strongest link in the chain, '[pretending] that their whole argument is rigorous because this one link is' (p. 7). The attention devoted to the strongest links has left weaker links, and the chain as a whole, in severe distress. In exalting precision and rigour in selected parts, economists forsake truth and relevance in the whole. Model-building often can 'deal only with part of the problem' (p. 7).

Mayer's 'principle of the strongest link' conforms nicely to McCloskey's lamppost metaphor: 'the extreme explicitness of modernist reasoning under the lamppost is accompanied by extreme vagueness outside its range' (McCloskey, 1990: 73). To repeat, McCloskey's lamppost parable should be revised: the Everyman seeks the lost keys and the nincompoop libertarian economist refrains from showing him where they are. Using either the revised McCloskey parable or Mayer's metaphor, we may characterise a 'public discourse' orientation for the economics profession.

A public discourse orientation asks that: (a) when appropriate in their academic work, economists get beyond the light of the lamppost, using flashlights, cigarette lighters or mirrors placed under the lamppost to reflect its light, to come up with the lost keys, *and* (b) economists take the trouble to show the Everyman where the lost keys are. To put it in terms of Mayer's metaphor: a public-discourse orientation calls for economists to: (a) mind the strength of the entire chain of argument in their academic work, *and* (b) help the Everyman understand their chains of argument.

Points (a) and (b) go naturally together. If economists mind their entire chains of argument, they will naturally be drawn into the specifics of government policy, bringing them close to the Everyman; furthermore, many of the links in the chain will not be susceptible to formalisations; to work on those links economists will have to proceed in a mode fitting their own experience and intelligence as an Everyman. If economists are addressing the Everyman, they will have to offer entire chains of argument. They will be scorned if they offer only a few disconnected links, even if those links are very strong.

The rival orientation is scholasticism (not to be confused with scholarship or scholarliness). In the scholastic orientation, economists are scientists and they may neglect the Everyman, focusing instead on what the profession officially deems worthy. Again, Stigler (1982: 34, 66-7; 1988: 85, 179) and Rosen (1997: 151) espouse such an orientation. In practice, this orientation tends towards the principle of the strongest link. In a scholastic profession, it will never be academically (or, in Stigler's language, 'scientifically') rewarding to do excellent public policy work that is useful to the Everyman. As has been noted, weak links in the Everyman's chain of reasoning call not for scholastic crafts, but a sensible and informed use of basic economic insights and low-tech forms of evidence.

My interpretation echoes Smith's interpretation of the universities and churches of his own time. Smith (1776) said that institutions subsisting on endowments or state support tend to lose enthusiasm for the basic instructional needs of the people (p. 740). University faculties become a self-evaluating body and indulge each other's neglect of basic teaching (p. 718). Instead they occupy themselves with elegant yet arid learning (pp. 727, 741). Furthermore, their avoidance of 'the current opinions of the world' shields their own beliefs from challenge. Many universities '[have remained], for a long time, the sanctuaries in which exploded systems and obsolete prejudices found shelter and protection, after they had been hunted out of every other corner of the world' (p. 727). Smith's discussion of universities suggests that in scholastic communities irrelevance and bad judgement go together.

8 A MODEL OF PREFERENCE FALSIFICATION WITHIN THE ECONOMICS PROFESSION

The problem within economics is similar to the spread and persistence of Affirmative Action and Socialism. Timur Kuran (1995) has developed a theory of 'preference falsification'. Individuals have private preferences about a public matter, such as whether the economics profession should be more public-discourse oriented. But the individual may choose to display publicly a preference contrary to his private preference: 'The reason our individual might opt for preference falsification is that his public preferences influence how he is valued and treated. To maintain acceptance and respect, he must provide evidence that he accepts society's basic institutions and shares its fundamental objectives and perceptions' (p. 26).

Academics know about falsifying one's preferences:

> Some public preferences elicit disapproving gestures, such as raised eyebrows and derisive stares. . . . A person considered on the wrong side of an issue may be denied a job . . . On the positive side, a person may receive various benefits for an expressed preference. The possible rewards include smiles, cheers, compliments, popularity, honors, privileges, gifts, promotions, and protection. (Kuran, 1995: 29)

The problem may be represented in a model introduced by Thomas Schelling (1973). Figure 3 treats as a population the more

Figure 3 **At point A no one supports public discourse and everyone is worse off**

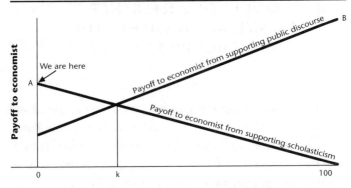

Percentage of economists supporting public discourse

libertarian sector of professional economists. Each chooses a public display of professional support for *either* a public-discourse orientation *or* a scholastic orientation. The economists within that population (itself a subset of the profession) are assumed to have the same payoff functions and to prefer a public-discourse orientation for the population as a whole. The vertical axis measures individual payoff and the horizontal axis measures the percentage of the group supporting public discourse. When no other economists support public discourse, the individual's payoff from supporting public discourse is less than his payoff from supporting scholasticism. Point A is a stable equilibrium in which everyone falsifies his preference. This is a tragedy, morally and socially. The other stable equilibrium is point B, where everyone expresses his private preference for public discourse. Everyone is better off.

The more libertarian sector of academic economics in America is stuck at point A. However, if enough economists, corresponding to threshold k, were to co-ordinate a shift in orientation, things might change. Schelling suggests how the k group might succeed:

> More selective groupings . . . can organize incentive systems or regulations to try to help people do what individually they wouldn't but collectively they may wish to do. Our morals can substitute for markets and regulations, in getting us sometimes to do from conscience the things that in the long run we might elect to do only if assured of reciprocation. (Schelling, 1978: 128)

If a k group were to organise, then others might follow rapidly. Indeed, Kuran explains many momentous changes as the rapid unravelling of preference falsification. As Mayer (1993) puts it: 'Recent events suggest that a hollow ideology is not likely to endure' (p. 4).

9   CONCLUDING REMARKS

The plea for a public-discourse orientation is a plea for reform at the margin (in this respect Figure 3 might be misleading). A scholarly community depends on standards for good research, and those needs are relatively well met by equilibrium model-building and statistical significance. Not only are modelling and statistics great blessings, but a degree of scholasticism is inevitable and indeed desirable. But there is *too much*. I ask economists to relax certain scholastic norms, to foster research and teaching that is less paradigmatic and more policy relevant. In Figure 4, such a shift is represented by a move from point A to point B.

In good policy-relevant work, the chains of argument are usually made up of links even the strongest of which are not very fancy. Economists might shift their standards to the evaluation of entire chains of policy argument, not just the strongest links. Policy-relevant work is bound to involve greater exercise of judgement, and ideology will be more pronounced. Smith and the classical economists expressed a 'forthright concern with fostering the sociopolitical forces that spark and sustain [the process of competition]' (Machovec, 1995: 9).

A return to judgement would be desirable. Economists tend to see consensus as the hallmark of science, but in a science like political economy, where the true practitioner is the Everyman, perhaps equal standing should be given to *dialogue*. Judgement, like

Figure 4 **Economists can increase society's utility by finding a different balance between public discourse and scholasticism**

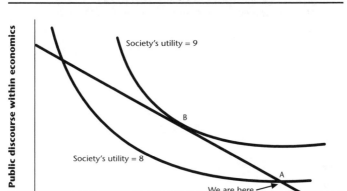

Scholasticism within economics

Scotch, is heady stuff. But one may learn to imbibe more responsibly and to tolerate better the passions of other imbibers. I ask economists to make their seminar rooms and professional journals more open to policy debate and outspokenness.

The passages lately quoted from Kuran say that individuals face external incentives in choosing their social conduct. But Kuran writes also of the internal value that people feel in doing what they think is right. Adam Smith also wrote of this, and his words help to explain why the economics profession produces as much good research, and exercises as much good influence on public affairs, as it in fact does today:

> Nature, accordingly, has endowed [man], not only with a desire of being approved of, but with a desire of being what ought to be approved of ... [T]hough a wise man feels little pleasure from praise where he knows there is no praise-

worthiness, he often feels the highest in doing what he knows to be praise-worthy, though he knows equally well that no praise is ever to be bestowed upon it. (Smith, 1790: 117)

COMMENTARIES

1 John Flemming

I agree with most of Daniel Klein's analysis and argument but with some differences of emphasis, prescription and hope.

There are at least four distinct and perfectly legitimate economic products:

(i) theoretically rigorous exploration, testing the validity and limits of propositions already in circulation;

(ii) academic empirical studies collecting new data on which to base new propositions or test existing hypotheses or to assess their empirical relevance;

(iii) studies applying established techniques to the evaluation of particular policies or projects; and

(iv) policy debate applying established principles of liberty, democracy and economic welfare to major strands of policy and also to particular instances.

Klein's argument is that not enough resources are devoted to the final category – he also suggests that the other categories are less infused by the Smithian elements of the last than they might be.

It can also be argued that to the extent that the norm is liberal the ingenious exceptions generated by innovative treatments are liable to be given an anti-liberal spin – if they have any influence on applications at all.

It may be true that there is a trade-off between relevance/importance and rigour/precision, confronted with which too many economists incline to the latter, but I think this is a minor point relative to the respective incentives for the four different types of product.

To the extent that I am conscious of the trade-off it is not a matter of marginal adjustment. When one makes an unrealistic or restrictive assumption in order to find a tractable formulation from which possibly spurious explicit results can be obtained, the only alternative is hand-waving assertion. A problem is either tractable or intractable to the economist working on it. It is not true that a slightly lesser willingness to sacrifice realism or relevance would produce a slightly less rigorous solution – one would get no explicit solution at all. Economic theorists in fact pursue generality and love to be able to say that they can make some assumptions 'without loss of generality'.

I therefore prefer to focus on the incentives to produce each of the four products distinguished above. While the first may enjoy some edge of prestige over the second, they are both clearly 'academic', whereas much of the third category of work is undertaken by consultants and the last is liable to be dismissed as being journalistic because it is aimed at a non-professional audience.

Indeed, one of our problems is that of specialisation that reduces communication between professional economists in different fields: theory or econometrics, money or public finance, international trade or labour markets. Each of these, and many more, areas has its own devotees who rarely stray outside its confines as a reader, let alone as a writer.

The incentive to work as or for consultants is largely financial, and in the UK at least the financial pressures on academics have made them increasingly susceptible to such inducements, reducing time for other kinds of contribution. Equally important, and possibly more pernicious, are the pressures of the UK Research Assessment Exercise which, at least hitherto, has given no credit to contributions to debates designed to reach Everyman.

In fact the RAE has increased pressure to do academic research, to publish, and to some extent to substitute quantity for quality. I know of a recent case in which a referee said of a submission to a journal that the author was profligate with ideas and should be advised to spread the material over several articles to gain more RAE points.

Thus the pressures and inducements to do other things than to engage in debate have increased; what of those to enlighten policymakers and influence public policy? There are several research institutes dedicated to such activities, and there are grant-giving bodies, both public and private, that promote policy relevance, accessibility and dissemination. There are also 'think-tanks' that take these matters to an extreme of shrillness that may deter the less partisan.

The rewards of writing for the general reader remain those of recognition and of influence. While these still exist they have probably not increased. Very few British newspapers carry serious contributions of that kind now – and to be heard one has to shout very loud. It is perhaps unsurprising that few are willing and the doubts of colleagues have increased.

What, of course, is possible is to post things on the web, either on one's own website, in an exchange site, or through the site of a newspaper. I am afraid that I have not done the research necessary to ascertain the scope of that medium. My suspicions are, however, rather discouraging. Everyman is probably not a keen seeker after such material on policy issues; in the past a relatively passive or habitual reader of a serious newspaper could be reached through its pages. Websites are likely to be dominated by the relatively obsessive and to offer little scope for the rewards of either general recognition or influence.

Thus I share Daniel Klein's wish for change but hold out little hope that the tide is running our way rather than in the opposite direction, even if liberal and pro-market ideas still get a better hearing today than a generation ago.

2 Charles Goodhart

The last two centuries have seen, as Martin Wolf noted in the *Financial Times* (6 September 1999), a continuing battle between command-and-control and market mechanisms for organising society. On this battlefield, it has been the economists who have devised and honed the intellectual weapons, even if it has been political leaders, from dictators to liberal democrats, who have put them into use. As Keynes said, 'Practical men, who believe themselves to be exempt from any intellectual influences, are usually the slaves of some defunct economist.'[1]

With Karl Marx on one side, Hayek and Friedman on the other, and Keynes as a middle way in between, the ideas of economists have been beacons for their myriad followers. You will recall the story of the Soviet military parade, with weapons of ever-increasing mass destruction, cumulating in a small van containing some men in grey suits. 'Who are they?' asked an onlooker; 'Economists,' was the response. 'But why?'; 'You should see the destruction and havoc they can cause.'

Clinton was supposed to have claimed that his election campaign had to have a major focus – 'It's the economy, stupid.' When a presidential candidate in the USA, or a party leader in most G7 countries, approaches elections, he or she will now usually have individual economists as advisers and economic programmes to put before the electorate. Leading politicians will also have scientific advisers, but scientific issues are rarely as electorally crucial as economic ones. I find it hard to believe that economics, and economists, do not figure sufficiently prominently on the public scene.

---

1   J. M. Keynes, *The General Theory of Employment, Interest and Money*, Macmillan, 1936, p. 383.

Nor are such economists always behind-the-scenes *éminences grises*. When I observe the role of Larry Summers, Stan Fischer or Joe Stiglitz, to name but a few, I do not feel that economists are shrinking violets constructing complicated formulae in ivory towers. Moreover, the recent trend towards giving central banks operational independence to set interest rates, so as to achieve an objective for price stability mandated by the politicians (and hence indirectly by the electorate), has led numerous economists to shift from a purely advisory towards a more directly decision-making mode. There is currently a majority of academically trained professional economists on the Bank of England's Monetary Policy Committee.

The claim made by Martin Anderson, cited by Daniel Klein, that, in his four-year experience, not once, 'in countless meetings on national economic policy, did anyone ever refer to any article from an academic journal' would not be representative of the Monetary Policy Committee (MPC). Indeed, I wonder whether Stigler's pronouncement, that academics should stick closer to their academic and theoretical last, and spend less effort on 'preaching', that is on policy advice, was partly driven by a feeling that too many economists were spending too much of their time in such exercises. Moreover, different schools of political ideology can always find some academically trained 'economists' to support their view. Since the public airwaves are filled with the rival claims of 'experts', Stigler may have felt that the basic *métier* of a serious economist lay in sorting out truth from falsehood, not in providing columns of instant advocacy in journalistic media.

Again, a considerable number of Klein's worries may be particularly related to more narrow US concerns. The US is a huge country, physically as well as economically, and Washington is a

very specialised community. I would guess that the average economist, including – perhaps *especially* including – the representative
macroeconomist, feels far more divorced from government circles
in the USA than she would in, say, Sweden, Spain, Italy or the
Netherlands. In some European countries it has at times appeared
that sound advice from macroeconomists in central banks, such as
the Banca d'Italia or the Banco de España, has helped those countries overcome periods of severe political weakness.

Economists in the USA, especially in academic centres outside
the North-East, seem to regard government, especially the federal
government in Washington, as a much more distant, alien, even
dangerous body than do economists in smaller European countries. Most senior economists in Europe can, if they should want to
do so, choose to play an engaged and in many cases influential role
in their own country's policies. The corridors of the Ministry of
Finance or of the Central Bank are not a dangerous *terra incognita*
to them as they seem to be to many in the USA.

I see no lack whatsoever of engagement in public-policy
debates on the part of economists in Europe, and I rather doubt
whether there is any such deficiency in the USA either. I do wonder
to an extent whether it could be argued that the commanding
leadership of US economists in the development of theory could
be ascribed to their generally greater divorce from policy advice
(and politics). But in the decades when the UK (or Sweden or
Austria) were the theoretical leaders, those theorists such as
Keynes, Robertson and Hawtrey were hardly divorced from policy
involvement (rather the opposite). A more compelling case for US
academic leadership in economic theory can be ascribed to
relative pay levels (in a competitive world market) and to
hysteresis. Indeed, it may be partly the rewards and excitement of

direct policy involvement which have managed to keep many of the remaining good (marketable) macroeconomists from joining the brain-drain across the Atlantic (or Pacific in the case of the Japanese).

Nor do I believe that liberal economists, who advocate more reliance on market mechanisms and less on government intervention, have been less willing to join in public-policy discussions (in 'preaching') than their more socialist colleagues. In particular, the shift from the view, or belief, that governments would altruistically seek to maximise the social welfare of the public to the view, or belief, that they are primarily concerned with an agenda of their own – in which sticking to power is usually predominant – has made enormous strides in recent decades. This has been due not only to the analysis but also the 'preaching' of liberal economists such as Buchanan and Tullock. It is, no doubt, partly a reflection of my having been trained at Cambridge (in both the USA and UK), but my own view is that the extent of cynicism about the motives of governments and their officials, for example as incorporated in the time inconsistency analysis, has gone too far. The pendulum certainly needed to swing from the idealistic view of government action widely held in the 1950s and 1960s, but my subjective assessment is that it has swung too far, driven largely by the successful 'preaching' of liberal economists.

Again, in the field of financial regulation, and intervention, for example, by central banks acting as lenders of last resort (where I have a professional interest), there is great pressure to restrict such actions, generally using the claim that any attempt to protect commercial institutions from their own folly will cause 'moral hazard'. The idea that moral hazard is at all times and everywhere a major disadvantage of intervention has been advanced with great success by the 'preaching' of liberal economists, without in my view any great empirical backing.

Overall my impression is that liberal economists have done rather well in the battle for the public ear in recent decades, as compared with their colleagues who might prefer more intervention. But I do not know how either participation, or success, in the battle for the public's attention can be measured. Since every believer in an ideology (and we all believe in various ideologies) believes that her own faith is the true faith, there must be a bias towards thinking that its failure to achieve universal adoption must relate to poor presentation and insufficiently good 'preaching'. My own view is that Dan Klein's paper is affected by just such an in-built bias. Liberal economists, in my view, can be proud of their preaching abilities.

Let me turn next to the other strand of Klein's critique, which is that, when academic economists retreat from the field of public-policy involvement, they turn, in their ivory towers, to the construction of analysis that is too formal, mathematical, rigorous and abstract. I have some limited sympathy with this view, especially in those cases where the maths is more complex and the theory more abstractly formal than can usefully be applied to the underlying empirical database.

Let me try to explain. Few people would describe the Black/Scholes formula for pricing options as a dirt-simple piece of maths. Nor would the maths necessary to try to reconstruct the probability density function of asset price expectations from option prices be regarded as easy or trivial. Yet these, and several other examples, involve the appropriate application of maths, rigour and precision to an accurate and large-scale database (of asset prices in spot, forward and derivative markets).

Again, when I was a younger official at the Bank of England, risk management was thought to be almost entirely a matter of practical experience, and financial regulation more a question of seeing what was done in the most respected institutions and copying it. Economists were not then generally welcome in supervisory departments. Now we have the application of mathematical analysis, such as risk metrics, to the analysis of such problems. Extreme value theory, and other quite complex analysis, is being increasingly and appropriately applied.

But the ability to use maths techniques and precision successfully and usefully does depend on an adequate database. Will it be possible to develop credit-metrics effectively, if the loan-loss experiences of each bank are regarded as purely confidential data, not to be more widely shared? The path-breaking Miller-Orr analysis of the demand for money several decades ago rested on their access to confidential data on money balances from one single firm. The failure of demand-for-money analysis to develop much further is due in some large part to the treatment of such data on money balances as 'confidential'. Much of the advance in our understanding of the functioning of the foreign exchange market has come from the access of one economist, Professor Richard Lyons, to the deals for a fairly short period of time of one (anonymous) fx trader!

Where the data allows, as in many financial markets, the application of rigour, precision and maths has been remarkably fruitful. Another example in the same vein is the work by Paul Klemperer on auction theory. The difficulty arises when we move from the micro-analysis of markets to macroeconomics. Here the data are limited and inaccurate. Most economists do not realise how inaccurate (and often collected and aggregated in ways that are sub-optimal) these data are. The macro outcomes are the result of the interaction of millions of heterogeneous people, each with their own limited information set and prior beliefs. The attempt to formalize such a complex system by making simplifying assumptions, such as representative agents (e.g. a representative producer) or common knowledge of the true model of the working of the economy (a strong form of rational expectations), goes so far beyond what can be justified, or tested against the data, that it does often lead to a feeling that the resulting models involve empty formalism.

Douglass North claims that: 'The rationality assumption that has served economists and all the social scientists well for a limited range of issues in macroeconomic theory is a devastating shortcoming in dealing with most of the major issues confronting social scientists and policy-makers, and it is a major stumbling block to the path of future economic progress.'[2]

I tend to agree with North. The basic problem is that the fundamental constraint on humans is time, not money or wealth. We can never begin to learn everything relevant to our own discipline, let alone other disciplines. We all have to make choices over rationing our own time, for example consciously *not* to become expert in many fields; foreign languages, electronics and the internal combustion engine, to name but three in my own case. The vast majority of people make similar choices to exclude expertise in macroeconomic modelling and portfolio management, for example; and that choice – given their occupations and position – will be entirely rational. When we know that we do not know much

---

2   Douglass C. North, *Understanding the Process of Economic Change*, Institute of Economic Affairs, Occasional Paper 106, 1998.

about a subject, we ask what others are doing and we seek help from a variety of 'experts', some valid, others less so.

Under such conditions, of limited time and partial learning, the likelihood of such phenomena as herding, cascades, bubbles, etc., becomes large. Market outcomes, especially in asset markets, are likely to be volatile and at times inefficient. This should not be taken to be a covert argument in favour of more intervention, because public-sector actions also have serious handicaps, for example bureaucracy, buck-passing, attempts at voter manipulation, potential corruption, etc. The fact that the market outcome is imperfect does not, *ipso facto*, mean that the command-and-control outcome is any better – far from it.

What I do believe, however, is that the real world is one in which rationality is inevitably bounded by time constraints and where individuals are (thankfully) all very different. Trying to force models (in the interests of some abstract rigour) into a set mould of fully rational expectations, representative agents and perfect markets drives the results so far from reality that the outcome is a formal rhetoric without contact with practical policy issues. Put another way, Lucasian macro-models have, not surprisingly, had virtually zero impact on macro-policymaking. That would be so whatever the extent of maths used to embellish the models with technical virtuosity.

Two defences, at least, may be offered. The first is that attempts to make macro-models more realistic by taking into account bounded rationality, learning processes, heterogeneity, etc., are so difficult that it is right to start with simpler, though less realistic, models that at least have a rigorous, 'deep', intellectual basis. But in the meantime practical policymakers are actually going to stick with the kind of extended Keynesian structural models that Lucas criticised so strongly decades ago. The alternative, a more 'rigorous', macro-modelling approach preferred by academics for their journal articles, largely fails the test of practical usage so far when policymakers (in some cases those same academics under another hat) seek empirical support for their necessary decisions.

The second defence is that these more formal, 'rigorous', Lucasian models can be, and are, confronted with the data via the new empirical exercise of 'calibration', that is seeing whether the main economic characteristics of an artificial world driven by the model appear 'close' to that of the real world. In my view 'calibration' is rather closer to a simulation exercise than to standard econometric hypothesis testing. Simulation, and I would expect also calibration, usually make the research worker feel that he/she has really learned something of considerable value about the real world, but rarely manage to impress the outside reader.

There are, of course, exceptions, especially where calibration points up real-world features that seem grossly at odds with the models, the equity premium puzzle being the best known (that is, why have equities yielded so much more than other financial assets when their relative riskiness is not so much greater?).

Let me now conclude. There are many areas of economics in robust good health. Here hypotheses are derived from past theory, observation and intuition and then tested against the data. The results of such empirical tests lead to revision of the hypotheses, and so on. The mathematical and econometric techniques applied are those which the researcher needs to resolve the problems. Most of finance, much of the study of individual markets and most of microeconomics seem to me to meet those standards.

Macroeconomics is, of course, much more difficult. The database remains grossly insufficient (partly because of excessive concerns about confidentiality, which has remained a baleful influence on academic advances throughout economics), and far more inaccurate than most economists realise. We cannot undertake controlled experiments. Even if we could, individuals learn from such outcomes and adapt their behaviour. The alternatives range between rough-and-ready regression exercises without much theoretical basis (of which simple Vector Auto-Regressions, VARs, are an extreme form) to formal models which introduce an abstract, 'deep', theoretical purity at the expense of institutional reality. None of the above approaches has much claim to be 'scientific'.

3 Israel M. Kirzner

Professor Daniel Klein has presented a passionate, eloquent plea for economists who favour liberty to engage in 'concrete policy work' rather than in 'fancy models and fancy econometrics'. In this way, Klein argues, economists can engage in public discourse, and will be far more likely to influence public policy for the better. Klein sharpens his sermon to libertarian-minded economists by contrasting his position with that of the late George Stigler, the eminent Nobel Prize-winning economist, who believed that economists, *qua* economists, have no business telling the public what to do (since, Stigler believes, the public already knows everything worth its while to know). For Stigler, the economist who attempts to affect public policy is (deplorably, in Stigler's opinion) 'preaching'; that is, he wishes to alter the public's view of what is good for it. This, Stigler believed, is not something which the economist, as scientist, has any right to do. As scientist he can certainly engage in the communication of knowledge and information. But since the public must, Stigler believed, be treated as already knowing all the relevant information worth knowing, there is really nothing worthwhile which the economist can teach the public. The economist who speaks to the public is either 'preaching' or wasting his own time and that of the public.

Klein's thesis, sharply disagreeing with Stigler, thus consists of (a) a positive claim, and (b) the assertion of a moral imperative. The positive claim is that the attention of the public (and thus, indirectly, of the makers of public policy) can be grabbed – not by rarefied theoretical work, but by down-to-earth applied, policy-oriented economics. The moral imperative which Klein asserts is that economists who believe in a free society have – *contra* Stigler – a moral duty to influence policymakers for the better, and therefore, as established in the 'positive claim', had better renounce 'fancy models and fancy econometrics' in favour of more relevant and important (if less rigorously precise) concrete policy work. If Klein's case were confined strictly to these two propositions, this writer could gladly declare himself in agreement with both of them; with the positive claim, and (subject to a presumption to be stated below) with the asserted moral imperative. Unfortunately, however, in developing his case Klein has needlessly confused his position by unnecessarily injecting additional ideas which, if accepted, would in fact not at all strengthen the overall message projected in his paper but, on the contrary, would seriously undermine the successful transmission of that message.

Klein's above-cited two propositions are easy to accept. That the eyes of policymakers (let alone those of the public at large) glaze over when they encounter the pages of today's mainstream economic journals is hardly news (and is well documented in Klein's paper). That Klein's asserted moral imperative is valid, given his premises, is as obvious as the assertion that a physician, observing a human being about to ingest a liquid which (unbeknown to that human being) medical science knows to be likely to induce a fatal disease, has a moral duty to inform – nay, to persuade – that individual concerning the dangers involved in drinking the liquid. An economist who is himself convinced concerning the real dangers to society implied by government interventionist policies unquestionably has a moral duty – of course, a duty the priority of which must be judged in the context of other relevant moral obligations incumbent upon the individual economist – to speak out to the relevant decision-makers concerning those dangers. Were Klein to confine his argumentation to the above, we could applaud the perceptiveness and the moral acuity of his position in this fine paper. Unfortunately, however, Klein is not content with the above.

Klein argues his case not merely by exhorting economists to inform (or to persuade) the public concerning the knowledge which economic science can provide, but, most importantly, by exhorting economists to exercise their influence, as do parents on their children, to change the values of the public (p. 35). Economists should not take the interests of the members of society as given and fixed; they should 'provide guidance about *what their listeners' interests should be*' (ibid.; italics in original). It is here that one fears that Klein has gone too far – in fact he has, this writer submits, gone astray.

Klein rightly observes that the moral duty of a liberty-loving economist to speak out on policy derives to a considerable extent from the reputation for truthfulness which the economist enjoys. It is precisely because his reputation guarantees a respectful hearing that the economist has a moral obligation to speak out. In Klein's words, when 'an economist argues against licensing restrictions, the argument persuades because of its logical cogency and factual support, but also because it comes from a sincere, scrupulous and capable economist'. This writer submits that if the economist deliberately goes beyond teaching members of society what policies will promote their welfare as they see that welfare, and proceeds to attempt to persuade them to give up what they believe to be in their deepest interests (in favour of what the economist believes to be in their deepest interests), the economist will rapidly lose the very reputation for scrupulous disinterestedness which now provides at least part of the basis for the validity of Klein's asserted moral imperative.

When Stigler, in his sermon against what he viewed as preaching by economists, called upon economists to stop addressing the public, he was indeed wrong. But he was wrong not because economists, in their capacity of economists, should be preaching (in the sense of seeking to persuade listeners to change their own deepest moral rankings), but because it is not necessary for economists, in their capacity of economists, to preach at all. Economists have information and insights, based on 'logical cogency and factual support', which they can communicate to the public without preaching to the public (in the sense of seeking to have it rethink its deepest values). (The reader should not misunderstand me: certainly every seasoned teacher knows that to teach calls for the art of persuasion (those same arts required for successful preaching), but there is a fundamental difference between (a) persuading (teaching) a listener as to which is the shortest way to get to point B from point A, and (b) persuading that listener that B is a morally preferable place in which to live than A. To persuade, in the sense of successfully transmitting a logical argument or factual information, is to teach. And the art of teaching does often call for the wiles of Madison Avenue. So long as what is being transmitted is a matter of demonstrable logic or fact, such persuasion is still 'teaching'. On the other hand, to persuade, in the sense of changing the deepest values of the listener, is to preach. One may indeed have a moral duty to preach. This is true for the scientist as it is for any human being; but it remains nonetheless true that preaching is simply not part of the activity of the scientist *qua* scientist.)

Our concern here is that, by exhorting the liberty-loving economist to preach in his role of economist the case for loving liberty as a pure value (rather than confining himself to his professional task of teaching how a free-market society can generate prosperity and the fulfilment of human goals), Klein is contributing to the erosion of that very aura of sincerity, scrupulous honesty and objectivity upon which the economist's professional influence with the public depends.

No one was a more passionate exponent of the case for the free market society than my remarkable teacher, Ludwig von Mises. Mises believed that the very survival of mankind depended on the economist's succeess in transmitting the teachings of economic science to the public. A glance at the closing paragraphs of Mises's monumental *Human Action* reveals the deep and passionate moral convictions which drove him to pursue his scientific career with an integrity that made him not merely unpopular but a virtual outcast in the mid-century economics profession (swept as it was by the interventionist fashions of the time).

In all this Mises was obeying precisely that very moral imperative which Klein has rightly emphasised in this paper. But, at the same time, no one was more emphatic than was Mises about the need for economists to adhere strictly to *wertfreiheit*; that is, to present their scientific conclusions, particularly their normative conclusions, in a way that takes account, not of the values held personally by the economist as a human being, but only of the goals of those to whom the economist is providing his professional advice. (To cite Mises as a shining example among exponents of *wertfreiheit* is not to deny that a good deal of his own scientific writing was unsuccessful in concealing the underlying moral passion which drove him, so that it misled many readers to see Mises as being not at all *wertfrei*!) Now, it is admittedly the case that many modern philosophers no longer accept (as this writer, at least as a practical matter, does accept) Mises's sharp distinction between the demonstrated conclusions of science on the one hand, and the expression of personal judgements of value on the other. Klein is certainly entitled to argue, *contra* Mises, that when people disagree on values they are ultimately disagreeing on matters of fact. But our deep concern for the potentially dangerous implications of Klein's thesis as he has presented it does not depend on the ultimate philosophical truth of Mises's distinction. Even if, at some level of philosophical determination, Klein's rejection of any categorical distinction between scientific propositions and judgements of value is decisively upheld, these implications remain fully as dangerous (for the very ideological positions which Klein holds dear, and which have motivated his paper) as we have shown them to be.

For the simple truth is that, regardless of philosophical argumentation to the contrary, the person in the street does agree with the Misesian-Weberian distinction. The public whom Klein is concerned to persuade does see a difference of kind between propositions which can, in principle, hope to command agreement among reasonable scientists, on the basis of conventional scientific criteria, and those other propositions (expressions of sheer personal conviction) which cannot.

Klein, the competent economist, exhorts his fellow economists, on moral grounds, to enlighten public policy through their scientific expertise. He is able to do so because he is a competent economist. But in engaging in such moral exhortation he is, of course, speaking not *qua* economist, but as the morally concerned citizen (deploying the results generated by science).

Klein is, rightly and righteously, preaching. But when Klein urges his fellow economists to seek, *qua* economists, to change the deepest interests of the public, he is urging them to muddy the line between their roles as scientists and their identity as morally concerned human beings. In so doing, one fears, Klein is encouraging economists to surrender the very reputation for sincerity and scrupulous objectivity upon which the potential influence of economists over the public depends.

4 Deirdre McCloskey

When I was a second-year assistant professor at the University of Chicago I heard a coffee-room dispute between Milton Friedman and George Stigler that made a great impression on me, and makes Daniel Klein's point. Milton was complaining about protection. George said (from a foot above: Milton is unusually short and George unusually tall; their tennis games on the court over at the Quadrangle Club were therefore a local sensation), 'Milton, you're such a preacher! If people wanted efficiency they could have it.' Milton replied, 'But people are misled. I want to teach them.' 'Teach! Don't waste your words.'

I was George Stigler's colleague for twelve years and can attest that Klein is correct in saying that Stigler believed 'the persuasive power of conversation is negligible'. It's a wonder that George wrote anything at all, so persuaded was he that Interest dominated Mere Words. Why bother 'preaching' against the errors of the Harvard School of monopolistic competition, for example, if the school's foundation in academic interest is so plain? They say what they say because the money's there, not because they are making arguments open to learning. Though George was a skilful arguer and one of the best stylists in economics (for what that commendation is worth), at a theoretical level he had no appreciation of Rhetoric. Adam Smith began his career teaching rhetoric to Scottish boys and ended making it the foundation of his ethical system. As Klein remarks, 'Austrian economics and Deirdre McCloskey', and Adam Smith and Milton Friedman, think differently. We think that words matter.

A long time ago Michael Oakeshott wrote that knowledge is information plus judgement. We are accustomed to viewing the amount of 'information' on the Internet with wonder or alarm.

Isn't it wonderful, this massing of information, 'at our fingertips', we say. But information unjudged is useless. The Moscow phone directory of old, it is said, was filled with errors. Using it required an exercise of judgement – textual criticism, say, that would emend a '34' to '43'; or a grasp of what sectors were likely to be more reliable than others. And even using the London directory, which we may assume is without blemish in the matter of sheer information, requires judgement. Whom do you wish to call? For what pragmatic purpose? With what persuasive intent? At what time of day? What *do* these numbers mean? A computer lacking common sense or socialisation would have no idea how to use such knowledge, because knowledge, with that element of judgement, is a human game, serving human meanings.

The point is simply that judgements and meanings are made within human speech communities. We 'make people willing to see certain basics' in economics *rhetorically*. And the rhetor, the good person skilled at speaking (as Quintilian put it), is just what Klein is recommending. We economists are skilled at making the simple, mixed fact-and-intellectual-tradition judgements most people miss: to mention the judgements I have made today reading the newspaper, that it is lunacy, for example, for Norwegian sheep farmers who produce $70 of product per sheep to be paid $200 of subsidy per sheep by Norwegian taxpayers to do it; that when non-Vietnamese artificial fingernail technicians in California complain about the non-FDA-approved ingredient used by the Vietnamese at half-price they are protecting their incomes, not the consumers; or that California freeways would have optimal congestion instead of the insane amounts they have now if they were not free.

I do not think Klein makes his case against 'fancy models and fancy statistical significance' quite explicit (it should be noted, to speak of *ethos*, that Klein himself is very well versed at least in fancy models, and can proffer irrelevant existence theorems with the best of them; so he speaks from knowledge, not ignorance). He may by inadvertence leave the impression that something is actually being accomplished of a scientific character in mainstream economics – though the word 'scholasticism' suggests he shares my doubt. My doubt is that anything much of value *scientifically* has come out of American academic economics since Samuelsonian economics took over the centre around 1950. I disagree that 'equilibrium model-building and statistical significance' are 'great blessings', at any rate in their Samuelsonian form: existence theorems plus statistical significance have been known for decades to have nothing whatever to do with scientific thinking. The nouvelle Chicago concession in the 1980s to theorem-provers in Stanford and Harvard has made the situation worse. Now, as Klein notes, nothing of value gets into journals of economics. I read a paper earlier today by a young economist who believed that the behaviour of medieval English peasants can be deduced, with no recourse to facts, from blackboard assumptions (for example, that the peasants loved each other and would help one of their number who fell on bad times).

My point is that the above-the-fray scholasticism that Stigler and his heirs at Chicago, such as Gary Becker and Robert Lucas, recommend is phoney as science. This despite their Nobel Prizes, God bless 'em. The emperor has no clothes. (Incidentally, people usually say it was a little *boy* in the Andersen story who made this observation. I have checked: the gender of the child is not actually specified. I prefer to think of it as a little *girl*, since females are more apt to see through male illusions than males are.)

So I agree with Klein, but would go even further in getting back to Adam Smith. We need people to take their courage in hand and start doing real economic science. *That* science will be policy-relevant, all right, as relevant as old Adam's unscientific books of 1776 and 1790.

5 Gordon Tullock

It is somewhat hard to respond to a paper that in general is in accord with your own reasoning but nevertheless disagrees with you firmly on at least one important point. I think an ambitious young economist would be well advised as a career move to engage in at least some efforts to improve policy by publishing or speaking to a non-economic audience. Klein disagrees.

He goes to the extreme of suggesting that anything of this sort be deliberately removed from the ambitious young economist's vitae. I do not think that is good advice, but I would suggest that such papers or speeches be segregated. Thus the vitae would contain a list of 'scholarly' articles and a second list of 'education', 'public relations' or 'policy-relevant' papers. This is not only worthwhile; it is more honest than putting all in one long list. Your vitae would still have the same number of pages, but the reader would realise that not all of them involved as much technical knowledge as the others. I think most employers would regard policy interest as a plus, even if not an overwhelming plus. Further, as I pointed out in that part of my speech Klein quoted, it is fairly easy to become an expert on such a subject. The expertise does not have to be original or profound. It is aimed not at the professional economist but at the voter, or perhaps the Congressman or local government.

The above is substantially my only difference with Klein. I do think the well-intentioned economist who spends some time in attempting to improve economic policy by addressing the common man, or even the government official, will benefit the world and will not injure his own career. Normally, however, these articles, speeches and even letters to the editor will not help him much in his career. I regard this as a serious criticism of the economic profession. The only reason for economics is to improve policy, mainly political policy, but to a minor extent policy followed by businesses.

To take an outstanding example, Henry Hazlitt was for many years the Economic Correspondent for the *New York Times*. During all this period, the *New York Times* opposed minimum wages. No doubt this was an example of his influence. When he retired, it became an advocate of minimum wages. Granted the influence of the *New York Times*, it seems likely that Hazlitt did more to improve economic policy than any five full professors of economics during this period. Nevertheless, he would not have been regarded as suitable for appointment in any leading university. No doubt he did well financially, and for that matter his popular books sold well. Nevertheless, the economic aristocracy never recognised him.

The rather low status of teaching, particularly elementary teaching, is indicative of the problem. Since, to make an embarrassing confession, I myself am not fond of teaching, I benefit from my high status. I have few classes and in general the students are good and interested. It is quite a different matter for those people teaching gigantic elementary courses. Nevertheless, from the standpoint of influencing future policy, the elementary teacher is more important than me. I hope that my work will trickle down to the elementary teacher and through him to the large number of potential voters, potential Congressmen and potential newspapermen in his class. This is, however, just my hope, though it is true that my writings are, generally speaking, much more accessible to the ordinary person than most economic writings.

Nevertheless, the present situation is in my opinion very undesirable. Economics is a policy science and we should be trying to influence policy. The vast output of the average economic journal contains little that would influence policy. By coincidence, I received my copy of the *American Economic Review* while preparing this comment. The general quality of the articles is, of course, excellent. Since it publishes only about 8 per cent of the articles it receives, that would be expected. Further, most of the articles have at least some policy relevance. The policy relevance, however, is usually small and to a considerable extent negated by the difficulty which a layman would have in reading them. Indeed, I would suspect that most teachers of elementary economics would regard the labour input from reading them as greater than the value they would derive.

From the standpoint of all-wise governments, subsidising policy-relevant research would be worthwhile. It would be particularly so if reinforced by further research suggesting changes in policy, or, in other (more frequent) cases, suggesting that existing policy be continued. Government, however, is not all wise. Only if information is digested and simplified will it have a policy effect. Moreover, there are additional problems. In addition to reading the *American Economic Review* I read the *Washington Post* and the *Washington Times* in order to get two views of political developments. Both of them not only carry many columns but also direct news. Some of the columns and some articles present correct economics. Others, however, would tend to mislead policymakers. It is not obvious that the policymakers can tell them apart.

Economic Affairs presents good economics, but there are other sources in the economic bookshops which tend to present plausible errors. On the whole, the average economist would have more policy influence writing letters to editors than articles for the *American Economic Review*. Unfortunately, as Klein points out, this would have a lower payoff under present circumstances. Nevertheless, the costs of production would also be less.

Currently, there is a debate at the popular level about various aspects of economic policy. I would like to have a much better debate. This means more policy-relevant articles of better quality. In this case, I cannot argue that the economic profession has failed because editorial decisions are not made by economists in the popular press.

I regret to say that, although I have thought about it carefully, I have no practical suggestions. Perhaps we could do something about the appointment and promotion process in the universities. The problem here is that any effort to change things is likely to get immediate bad publicity. Furthermore, experienced people in this area are normally pessimistic. There have been a number of cases in which money has been put up for the purpose of establishing new schools or endowing chairs, with the aim of carrying out the kind of research I am proposing, but the educational status quo has been too powerful. There is a newly founded university in Guatemala City which at least temporarily seems to have remained under the control of its original sponsors. How long all this will last is an open question.

So far I have mainly agreed with Klein. I now wish to turn away from him and then disagree with him in areas where he is more conventional than I. The articles that he refers to as 'rigorous' in my opinion frequently are not. There are two areas here – one is statistics and the other mathematics. Let me begin with statistics.

I was a student and friend of Karl Popper. Therefore I am strongly in favour of testing, which, in economics, frequently means statistical testing. Popper did not confine himself to that type of testing but he approved of it and made contributions to statistical theory. I follow him in this area, although my contributions to statistical theory are pretty trivial.

There are two basic problems here. The first of these is the significance test. Suppose, for purposes of illustration, we use .05

as our test. If we take a large number of potential bodies' data, at least one in twenty should show significant relationships, whether or not there is any true causal connection. What .05 means is that there is only a one-in-twenty chance that random data would have this close a relationship. Granted the number of tests performed and the fact that those which do not show significance are not even submitted to a journal, it is likely that those submitted to journals and published have a much higher probability than one in twenty of being chance relationships.

Richard Palmer has an article[3] on the subject in the *American Naturalist*. He emphasises that published articles are a subset of articles that were significant. Articles that do not have enough significance cannot be published, and an even lower-level problem is that the researchers will stop and shift to another topic if they do not get significant results. Thus the random occurrence of significant correlations should be much higher than one in twenty. This is not the whole problem, however.

There is then the sheer accident that correlation programmes are not identical. Most researchers simply use the one that is in their computer. Normally this makes little difference, but sometimes it does. More important, there is data torture. As Ronald Coase says, 'if you torture the data long enough it will confess'.[4] The young researcher, convinced he knows the truth, will make

---

3   A. Richard Palmer, 'Detecting Publication Bias in Meta-analyses: A Case Study of Fluctuating Asymmetry and Sexual Selection', *The American Naturalist*, vol. 154 #2, August 1999. I cite this instead of articles in the economic literature, including some of my own, because it is a very good article and shows we are not alone. Further, the problem in some ways is less severe in biology because there is more data and more control over the data. We use published data; biologists can create their own data and expand the data set at will.

4   I have heard him say this several times. So far as I know he has never published it.

changes in his model specifications and very likely produce significant results. In some cases this is correct; his original specification was wrong and his new one is right. Nevertheless, this procedure reduces the significance of the significance test.

Another problem is the data itself. Levy and Feigenbaum[5] have attempted to duplicate many statistical tests. In a few cases, the data seem to be either misreported or in some cases invented. The basic problem they discovered, however, is that it is very hard to duplicate many studies.

The reader is referred to their article[6] in *Social Epistemology* and to the more than fifty pages of comments on it (including one by this author) which follow it. Notably, no one denies the difficulty of duplicating statistical articles. Surely this raises questions as to whether they should be called rigorous.

Although this lowers the value of individual articles, I think that in bulk they support the theory. In a way, if 80 per cent of the articles' statistical tests are correct then the general theory is probably correct, and hence the correctly derived theoretical deductions in the other 20 per cent are probably right even if the statistical test is an artefact.

If the reader wishes to have his doubt of statistical research reinforced, I suggest he read the lengthy debate set off by Card and Krueger.[7] This is partly theoretical, but mainly a squabble about

---

5   'Testing the Replication Hypothesis: When the Data Set is Subject to Gross Error', *Economics Letters*, vol. 34 #1, 1990. Feigenbaum and Levy artificially introduced error into a body of statistics and tested its effect. With minor errors the effect was not fatal.

6   'The market for (ir)reproducible econometrics', *Social Epistemology: A Journal of Knowledge,Culture and Policy*, vol. 7 #3, July–September 1993.

7   D. Card and A. Krueger, *Myth and Measurement: The New Economics of the Minimum Wage*, Princeton University Press, 1996.

statistics. Once again, it raises questions about the use of the word 'rigorous' in discussing statistical work.

Let me now turn to mathematics in economics. Here I have no questions about the accurate nature of the work. Occasionally there are errors, but they are rare. The problem with mathematics in economics is that it is largely decorative rather than useful. Indeed, it is the opposite of useful since it makes articles that are basically simple hard to read.

Let me turn to experience of my own in connection with my first book, *The Politics of Bureaucracy*. Anthony Downs had been reading the manuscript and making helpful suggestions. In one part of the book, I discussed the tendency of information to be degraded as it goes up or down the administrative pyramid. For this purpose I used the compound interest formula. Downs commented that I could use calculus and in fact provided the necessary calculus. Needless to say, his calculus was impeccable. I did not use it because it seemed to me unwise to use more complicated tools than I needed. In essence he was proposing a decoration to my book. Much mathematics in articles on economics is similarly very decorative.

This decoration, by itself, would be harmless except that much of the work is designed to show that the author is right up with most recent and obscure developments in mathematics. Thus, although he makes no mistakes, this means that most people cannot read the article. Fortunately, in many articles the author begins or concludes by telling you in English what he is doing. Frequently, this is sufficient for it not to be necessary to read the rest. After all, one can be rigorous in English. Archimedes and Apollonius were rigorous in Greek and English is just as good. Still, a great many readers simply cannot follow mathematics. They are thus prevented from reading things which might have policy relevance.

Although this leads to a good deal of waste paper and hence ought to be opposed by environmentalists, its real cost is imposing a barrier of non-comprehension between people deciding on policy and those people best equipped to advise them. The question is, can we do something about it? Klamer and Colander[8] undertook a very interesting and non-mathematical study of graduate education in economics. Perhaps the most important result was that the graduate students did not like the overwhelmingly mathematical subject matter. Nevertheless, they thought they had to have a mathematical background to get a job. Probably they were right to believe this.

At the same time, undergraduates seem to be moving out of economics courses and hence reducing the demand for teachers. Some American universities have stopped teaching graduate economics. It is hard to say how far the rot will spread. It is, however, clearly a major problem, and I have to admit that I have no solution. One American university is considering changing its graduate programme to drop a great deal of mathematics. There are a couple of other departments that do not emphasise mathematics. Whether this effort will be successful I do not know.

Klein raises the problem but does not solve it. I regret to say that I cannot go farther than he has. It is a problem which should attract the best minds in economics. Unfortunately, they are mainly engaged in the type of research criticised by Klein and by me.

---

8   Klamer, Arjo, and David Colander (eds), *The Making of an Economist*, Westview Press, Boulder, 1990.

RESPONSE TO COMMENTARIES

Daniel B. Klein

The Everyman has always been the practitioner of political economy. The problem addressed by my paper is this: How do economists contribute to society when the practitioners are so rude in their understanding of economics? Economists have long struggled with the practitioner problem:

> Good Lord! What a lot of trouble to prove in political
> economy that two and two make four; and if you succeed in
> doing so, people cry, 'It is so clear that it is boring.' Then
> they vote as if you had never proved anything at all. (Bastiat,
> 1850: 11)[1]

In latter-day economics the practitioner problem entwines the professional problem of scholasticism and irrelevance. Hence I plead with economists. My plea attempts to enliven thought about the interlocking problems. I follow especially closely Deirdre McCloskey, except that my plea is directed only to economists with libertarian sensibilities. Because an economist's sense of calling is, in the final analysis, *not* separable from her political ideology, there is a niche for a discussion that proceeds upon my exclusionary presuppositions.

---

1   Bryan Caplan addresses the practitioner problem in a series of recent papers and introduces the term 'rational irrationality' as a companion to 'rational ignorance.' See Caplan (forthcoming).

My plea is similar to many since 1930. That my bottle of old wine (some would say *whine*) elicits a 'hear, hear' from leading classical-liberal economists heartens the author. To be commented on by John Flemming, Charles Goodhart, Israel Kirzner, Deirdre McCloskey and Gordon Tullock is a great honour. And the honour is redoubled by my being afforded a platform by an organisation (the IEA) that has grappled for generations, so gracefully, with the very problems being discussed.

I still say that Professor Tullock is innocent of how participating in public discourse and talking seriously about policy can injure one's standing with colleagues and the profession, maybe because he found a special niche in time, place and personality in which doing so, on the contrary, won him professional recognition. And I might disagree with Professor McCloskey's statements to the effect that modernist modes of discourse in economics have proven to be almost entirely barren. Mr Flemming suggests that making academic research more relevant would, contrary to what I suggest, involve more than marginal adjustment; here, I believe he is thinking of the individual piece of work, whereas I am thinking of the broad set of all works entertained professionally. His report on bureaucratic prejudice against Everyman discourse in Britain is distressing. As for his remarks about the Web as possible solvent, I am somewhat more optimistic, hoping that it will bring fragmentation and enable new modes of discourse and criticism.

I want to use the opportunity of rejoinder, however, to quarrel briefly with Professors Goodhart and Kirzner, and then elaborate on the economic profession's failure to deliver *oomph*.

Reply to Goodhart

Professor Goodhart mixes mild agreement with mild disdain. He rises above writing for non-economists: 'the basic *métier* of a serious economist lay in sorting out truth from falsehood, not in providing columns of instant advocacy in journalistic media.' But even when 'truths' are true, they aren't necessarily relevant or useful. Almost every theorem in the prestigious *Econometrica* is true but irrelevant to humanity. And writing for the Everyman ('instant advocacy') need not be (and ought not to be) irresponsible or sensationalist, of course.

Goodhart does not quite seem to face up to the Everyman problem, in which the truths wanting are often the very basic and relevant ones that the sound economist sorted out long ago (and are academically *infra*-marginal). The Everyman problem calls for us to be yeomen: 'We have to assert truths which to us seem obvious' (Mises, 1940: 233).

Estimating the extent of Everyman instruction, Goodhart notes: 'I see no lack whatsoever of engagement in public-policy debates on the part of economists in Europe, and I rather doubt whether there is any such deficiency in the USA either.' We might disagree over what 'engagement' means and what would constitute a 'deficiency'. But I would estimate that fewer than 5 per cent of economists at the 'top forty' departments publish per year one general-interest article (whether an op-ed, magazine article or policy study). That, to me, would be a lack of engagement.

To test my impression, I investigated the 1998 publications of the 112 authors who published in the 1998 *American Economic Review*. How many of them published in 1998 an article in a non-academic periodical (such as a newspaper, magazine, monthly or public-discourse-oriented quarterly)? I searched three electronic databases and found that five of the authors (or 4.5 per cent) had done so.[2]

Goodhart offers several examples of technical theoretical developments that have been fruitful. His examples all reside in Finance, but he could have pointed to canonical contributions in Political Economy (such as classic models of public goods, club goods, lemons markets, signalling, reputation, time inconsistency, path dependence and preference falsification). But I did not argue against *all* model-building. It is a question of proportions. Goodhart agrees that in macroeconomic work the proportions are faulty. I say the faultiness extends throughout the discipline.

Reply to Kirzner

Kirzner says that scientists should follow *wertfreiheit*: don't make value judgements; don't preach moral values; stick to logic and the facts.

However, the values that help to frame the logics and facts of a conversation can themselves be opened up to inquiry, and be

---

2   If we include Federal Reserve quarterlies, the *Monthly Labor Review* (published by the US Department of Labor), and the *NBER Reporter*, then the number goes up to twelve, or 10 per cent. The three databases I searched (during August 2000) were Academic Search Elite (which indexes 2,880 journals, more than 1,000 of which are not peer reviewed), Lexis-Nexis Academic Universe Major Newspapers (which indexes 58 leading newspapers), and Lexis-Nexis Academic Universe Magazines and Newspapers (which indexes hundreds of magazines and other non-academic sources). I searched for the names exactly as they appeared in the AER, so naturally my results are not precise. The five economists of the first group are (in alphabetical order) Kaushik Basu, Peter A. Diamond, Douglas A. Irwin, Peter Kuhn and Richard Schmalensee. The additional seven are Julian R. Betts, Michael R. Darby, Marvin Goodfriend, Randall S. Kroszner, Richard Rogerson, Katherine Terrell and Lynne G. Zucker.

treated as the logics and facts (so called) of larger inquiry. The logics and facts of Conversation 1 are found to rest on the deeper, supposed logics and facts of Conversation 2, and so on. An idea is a value (or end) in one discussion and an arguable piece of logic or fact (or means) in another. There is a cascade of ends, means, ends, means . . . We find that Conversation 1 and Conversation 2 are both parts of a single, greater conversation.

What are the values behind, say, support for a government school system? In arguing for government schooling, advocates may express their goal of creating a common school experience furnished by public, democratic institutions and making for a mutual, encompassing co-ordination of beliefs and sentiments. The focal points of such mutual co-ordination are official activities and texts, official ideas and stories. If that is the goal, if that is the value (and very often that *is* the value), the libertarian economist cannot retort that government schooling is not the best means of achieving it. Libertarian reforms, such as vouchers, will *not* serve that value. Instead, the libertarian economist must attack the value. By opening up a larger conversation about democracy, collective sentiments and government schooling, the libertarian economist digs up the beliefs or sentiments behind the value. The goal of encompassing collective experience is now treated as a *means*, and the libertarian economist suggests that it is a *bad* means to the array of broader and deeper social ends (whatever they may be: harmony, tolerance, joy, personal fulfilment, etc.). According to Kirzner, it would seem, libertarian scientists should patiently listen to schemes to advance fascist values. They may refrain from aiding such schemes, Kirzner seems to say, but ought not challenge the values presupposed. Here Kirzner agrees with Stigler (1982): 'Economists have no special professional knowledge of that which is virtuous or just' (p. 3). But neither does anyone else. I say libertarian scientists should aspire to explain the foolishness or selfishness of such values as fascism, collectivism, nationalism and coercive egalitarianism.

Kirzner might go along with me here but insist that once we get finally to the 'deepest values' of our listeners, we cannot and ought not challenge. Well, first, I did not propose the challenging of anyone's *deepest* values. Second, I am not sure we ever get to deepest values; we always seem to be able to find concerns and goals that go still deeper, or wrap around (see Hayek, 1960: 209). So, if Kirzner's objection to challenging values is confined to 'deepest' values, it is not really an argument against my paper, and if it is not so confined, it is not a valid argument.

Kirzner suggests that my plea jeopardises sincerity and scrupulous honesty. Being outspoken and exercising policy judgement need not, however, draw one into insincerity or dishonesty. Outspoken libertarian economists such as Smith, Say, Bastiat, Mises, Hayek, Hazlitt, Friedman, Buchanan, Tullock and Becker have displayed an admirable candour and intellectual integrity. Kirzner laments that Mises 'was unsuccessful in concealing the underlying moral passion which drove him'. Why lament the showing of passion?

Low-tech, high-*oomph* empirical evidence

Lest my paper be accused of favouring only armchair theorising and first principles, I elaborate here on how the basic argument applies as well to empirical evidence and argumentation.

What economists have to say is simple, says Coase (1975), yet the simple truths are commonly ignored in public-policy discussions.

Most economists do little to correct the lapse. They devote themselves to technical work that 'absorbs resources which might be devoted to . . . studies of the economic system of a nonquantitative character' (p. 45). Coase offers an example of low-tech, high-*oomph* theorising. Consider an official at the US Food and Drug Administration deciding whether to approve a new drug application. If he approves the drug and it turns out to be unsafe, he will be held up to public obloquy. If, instead, he declines approval he will avoid the risk of any such negative personal consequence. The logic suggests that the FDA will be too slow in approving drugs.

On the topic of the FDA, a small number of economists (and others) have produced *oomph*. I wish to extend Coase's example in the empirical direction by providing four arguments that FDA restrictions do little good and, given their tremendous costs, ought to be significantly reduced or even abolished. This argumentation serves as an example of empirical learning that the Everyman lacks and good economists could provide, but the structure of academic economics does little to encourage them to do so.

Quality and safety assurance without the FDA: four empirical arguments

Researchers can document very substantial morbidity and mortality from FDA restrictions. If voluntary society (plus the tort system) can provide assurance of quality and safety, the FDA is unredeemed. Here are four empirical arguments that voluntary society is up to the job.

(1) *Assurance in other industries.* How is safety assured in other industries? In electronics, manufacturers submit products to

Underwriters' Laboratories, a private organisation that grants its safety mark to products that pass. The process is voluntary: manufacturers may sell without the UL mark. But retailers and distributors usually prefer the UL mark. Private-sector institutions and the tort system assure safety in electronics.

(2) *Calamity prior to 1962?* The FDA was quite weak prior to 1962. The historical record – decades of a relatively free market up to 1962 – shows that free-market institutions and the tort system succeeded in keeping unsafe drugs to a minimum. The Elixir Sulfanilamide tragedy (107 killed) was the worst of those decades (Gieringer, 1985: 192). (Thalidomide did not reach the US.) The economists Samuel Peltzman (1973) and Dale Gieringer (1985) have made the grisly comparison: the victims of Sulfanilamide and other small tragedies prior to 1962 are insignificant compared to the death toll of the post-1962 FDA.

(3) *Were they dropping like flies in Europe?* All countries have their own counterpart to the FDA (just as they all have mail monopolies and agricultural handouts). But other countries do it quicker. From about 1970 to 1993 the approval times for drugs and devices in the United Kingdom, France, Spain and Germany was significantly shorter than in the US (although FDA drug approval times have improved and are now similar to those in Europe; Healy and Kaitin, 1999). The European agencies took less time to approve new drugs, but such laxness did not produce a scourge of unsafe drugs. As researchers of the Tufts Center for the Study of Drug Development write: 'the probability that a marketed drug will be removed for safety reasons was not appreciably greater in

the United Kingdom than in the United States' (Kaitin and Brown, 1995: 370). Lighter approval requirements did not lead to any noticeable problem. One explanation would be that the European agencies function more effectively (and there is reason to believe this). Another interpretation is that, in both Europe and the US, the government approval process, as a means of assuring safety, is *superfluous*.

(4) *The hidden lesson in off-label prescribing*. A drug's FDA-approved uses are called its 'on-label' uses. Once a drug is approved for any use, it passes through the FDA stranglehold and may be used in any way doctors and users see fit. Approved drugs are often found to have other beneficial uses, and doctors learn to prescribe drugs for such 'off-label' uses. The off-label uses have absolutely no standing with or approval by the FDA but are perfectly legal. Off-label prescribing is pervasive and vital to the health of millions of Americans. As economist Alexander Tabarrok (2000) says, 'most hospital patients are given drugs which are not FDA-approved for the prescribed use' (p. 25). Off-label prescriptions are especially common for AIDS, cancer and paediatric patients, but are common throughout medicine. Doctors learn of off-label uses from extensive medical research, testing, newsletters, conferences, seminars, Internet sources, and trusted colleagues. Scientists and doctors, working through professional associations and organisations, make official determinations of 'best practice' and certify off-label uses in standard reference compendia such as *AMA Drug Evaluations*, *American Hospital Formulary Service Drug Information*, and *US Pharmacopoeia Drug Information* – all without FDA meddling or restriction. Economist J. Howard

Beales (1996: 303) finds that off-label uses that later became FDA-recognised appeared in the *Pharmacopoeia* on average 2.5 years earlier. No one would be insensible enough to suggest that the FDA prohibit off-label prescribing. But, as Tabarrok astutely points out, there is a logical inconsistency in allowing off-label prescribing and requiring proof of efficacy for the drug's initial use. Logical consistency would require that one *either* (i) oppose off-label prescribing and favour initial proof of efficacy, *or* (ii) favour off-label prescribing and oppose initial proof of efficacy.

This is not the place to enlarge on the bane of drug restrictions; I have provided the empirical arguments in cursory fashion. I submit that anyone who dwelled seriously in this debate, with thinking held accountable to basic economics, would feel the *oomph*, really *know* the *oomph*, and become quite decidedly in favour of significant liberalisation.

None of the *oomph* depends on fancy research in 'top' journals. Tragically, the *oomph* is scarcely imparted to the Everyman. In fact, even among academic economists in the US, probably a majority are not much aware of the case against the FDA and harbour conventional fallacies about the matter. Academic economists are the Everyman first and good economists only maybe.[3]

The four arguments also suggest where good economists put their research efforts. It would be nice to have an economics profession in which papers such as Tabarrok's on off-label prescribing were published in top journals and regarded as

---

3   Here, what I mean, really, by 'good economist' is an economist with good policy judgement and sensibilities. That alone does not make one a good economist. There are many dimensions to being a good economist.

important contributions. Because such papers go relatively unrewarded, or even punished, economists producer fewer of them and deliver less *oomph* than they might.

But my aim is not primarily to tell 'top' editors that they should publish such papers (I do not suppose them to be listening). It is to invite the economists able to produce such papers to do so in spite of the fact that they will usually not be publishable in mainstream journals. If the good economists better assisted the Everyman and directed more research effort to *oomph* rather than to irrelevancies, society would be wiser, freer and more joyful.

Young economists, attending to their own academic security and survival, need help from the more established, older economists. By working together, the good economists rise above the meretricious academic concerns and invidious tendencies. They might alter the character of the economics profession as a whole, leading it to be more relevant and eventually wiser. In economics, relevance and good judgement form a virtuous circle.

Again, I thank Professors Flemming, Goodhart, Kirzner, McCloskey and Tullock for commenting on my paper.

REFERENCES

1 A Plea to Economists Who Favour Liberty

Anderson, Martin (1992), *Impostors in the Temple: American Intellectuals Are Destroying Our Universities and Cheating Our Students of Their Future*, Simon and Schuster, New York.

Boettke, Peter J. (1997), 'Where Did Economics Go Wrong? Equilibrium as a Flight from Reality', *Critical Review* 11, winter: 11–64.

Cannan, Edwin (1933), 'The Need for Simpler Economics,' *Economic Journal* 43, September: 367–78.

Cassidy, John (1996), 'The Decline of Economics', *New Yorker*, 2 December: 50–60.

Coase, Ronald H. (1975), 'Economists and Public Policy', in *Large Corporations in a Changing Society*, ed. J. Fred Weston, New York University Press, New York. Reprinted in Coase's *Essays on Economics and Economists*, University of Chicago Press, Chicago: 47–63. Reprinted in Klein, 1999B: 33–52.

Economist, The (1997), 'The Puzzling Failure of Economics', 23 August: 11.

Graham, Frank D. (1942), *Social Goals and the Economic Institutions*, Princeton University Press, Princeton.

Hamilton, Lee H. (1992), 'Economists as Public Policy Advisers', *Journal of Economic Perspectives* 6, summer: 61–64.

Hayek, F. A. (1944) (lecture), 'On Being an Economist'. First published in Hayek's *The Trend of Economic Thinking: Essays on Political Economists and Economic History*, ed. W. W. Bartley III and Stephen Kresge, University of Chicago Press, Chicago, 1991: 35–48. Reprinted in Klein, 1999B: 133–49.

Hayek, F. A. (1952), *The Sensory Order: An Inquiry into the Foundations of Theoretical Psychology*, University of Chicago Press, Chicago.

Hutt, W. H. (1936), *Economists and the Public*, Jonathan Cape, London. Reprinted 1990 (Transaction Publishers, New Brunswick). Pp. 34–7, 207–17 of the book are reprinted in Klein, 1999b: 53–68.

Ikeda, Sanford (1997a), *Dynamics of the Mixed Economy: Toward a Theory of Interventionism*, Routledge, London.

Ikeda, Sanford (1997b), 'How Compatible Are Public Choice and Austrian Political Economy? Tales of Deception and Error', mss. presented at the 1997 meetings of the Southern Economic Association.

Kirzner, Israel M. (1983), 'Does Anyone Listen to Economists?' (a review of George Stigler's *The Economist as Preacher and Other Essays*), *Inquiry: A Libertarian Review*, April: 38–40. Reprinted in Klein, 1999b: 125–31.

Kirzner, Israel M. (1985), *Discovery and the Capitalist Process*. University of Chicago Press, Chicago.

Klamer, Arjo, and David Colander (1990), *The Making of an Economist*, Westview Press, Boulder.

Klein, Daniel B. (1999a), 'Discovery and the Deepself', *Review of Austrian Economics* 11: 47–76.

Klein, Daniel B. (ed.) (1999b), *What Do Economists Contribute?*, Macmillan, London.

Knight, Frank H. (1951), 'The Role of Principles in Economics and Politics' (presidential address at the American Economic Association, 1950), *American Economic Review* 41, March. Reprinted in Knight's *On the History and Method of Economics* (1956), University of Chicago Press, Chicago.

Krugman, Paul (2000), 'In the Tank?', *New York Times*, 13 December.

Kuran, Timur (1995), *Private Truths, Public Lies: The Social Consequences of Preference Falsification*, Harvard University Press, Cambridge.

Machovec, Frank M. (1995), *Perfect Competition and the Transformation of Economics*, Routledge, London.

Mayer, Thomas (1993), *Truth versus Precision in Economics*, Edward Elgar, Aldershot.

McCloskey, Deirdre N. (1985), *The Rhetoric of Economics*, University of Wisconsin Press, Madison.

McCloskey, Deirdre N. (1990), *If You're So Smart: The Narrative of Economic Expertise*, University of Chicago Press, Chicago. Chapter 11 is reprinted in Klein, 1999b: 105–17.

McCloskey, Deirdre N. (1994), *Knowledge and Persuasion in Economics*, Cambridge University Press, New York.

McCloskey, Deirdre N. (1996), *The Vices of Economists, the Virtues of the Bourgeoisie*, Amsterdam University Press, Amsterdam.

Polanyi, Michael (1962), *Personal Knowledge: Towards a Post-Critical Philosophy*, University of Chicago Press, Chicago.

Roey, Stephen, Rebecca Rak Skinner, Rosa Fernandez, and Sam Barbett (1999), *Fall Staff in Postsecondary Institutions, 1997*, US Department of Education, Office of Educational Research and Improvement (National Center for Educational Statistics 2000–164), November.

Rosen, Sherwin (1997), 'Austrian and Neoclassical Economics: Any Gains from Trade?', *Journal of Economic Perspectives*, Fall: 139–52.

Schelling, Thomas C. (1973), 'Hockey Helmets, Concealed Weapons, and Daylight Saving: A Study of Binary Choices with Externalities', *Journal of Conflict Resolution*. Reprinted in Schelling, 1978: 211–43.

Schelling, Thomas C. (1978), *Micromotives and Macrobehavior*, W. W. Norton, New York.

Schelling, Thomas C. (1995), 'What Do Economists Know?', *The American Economist* 39, spring: 20–2. Reprinted in Klein, 1999b: 119–24.

Smith, Adam (1762), *Lectures on Rhetoric and Belles Lettres*, ed. J. C. Bryce, Oxford University Press, New York, 1983.

Smith, Adam (1776), *The Wealth of Nations*, Modern Library, New York, 1937.

Smith, Adam (1790), *The Theory of Moral Sentiments* (sixth ed.), ed. D. D. Raphael and A. L. Macfie, Oxford University Press, New York, 1976.

Solow, Robert (1999), review of *What Do Economists Contribute?*, *Eastern Economic Journal*, Fall: 481–3.

Stigler, George J. (1958), 'The Economies of Scale', *Journal of Law and Economics*, October. Reprinted in Stigler's *The Organization of Industry*, University of Chicago Press, Chicago, 1968: 71–94

Stigler, George J. (1961), 'The Economics of Information,' *Journal of Political Economy* 69, June: 213–25.

Stigler, George J. (1962), 'Information in the Labour Market', *Journal of Political Economy* 70, October: 94–105.

Stigler, George J. (1967), 'Imperfections in the Capital Markets',

Journal of Political Economy: 287–92.

Stigler, George J. (1976), 'The Xistence of X-Efficiency', *American Economic Review*, March: 213–16.

Stigler, George J. (1982), *The Economist as Preacher and Other Essays*, University of Chicago Press, Chicago.

Stigler, George J. (1988), *Memoirs of an Unregulated Economist*, Basic Books, New York.

Summers, Lawrence H. (1991), 'The Scientific Illusion in Empirical Economics', *Scandinavian Journal of Economics* 93(2): 27–39.

Tullock, Gordon (1984), 'How to Do Well While Doing Good!', an address delivered during the early 1970s at Virginia Polytechnic Institute. Published in David C. Colander (ed)., *Neoclassical Political Economy: The Analysis of Rent-Seeking and DUP Activities* (Ballinger Publishing Company, Cambridge, Massachusetts, 1984): 229–40. Reprinted in Klein, 1999b: 87–103.

Viner, Jacob (1927), 'Adam Smith and Laissez Faire', *Journal of Political Economy* 35, April: 198–232.

Wootton, Barbara (1938), *Lament for Economics*, George Allen and Unwin, London.

2 Response to commentaries

Bastiat, Frederic (1850), 'What Is Seen and What Is Not Seen', *Selected Essays on Political Economy*, ed. G. B. de Huszar, trans. S. Cain, Foundation for Economic Education, Irvington, New York, 1995.

Beales III, J. Howard (1996), 'New Uses for Old Drugs', *Competitive Strategies in the Pharmaceutical Industry*, ed. R. B.

Helms, American Enterprise Institute, Washington, DC: 281–305.

Caplan, Bryan (forthcoming), 'Rational Irrationality and the Microfoundations of Political Failure', *Public Choice*.

Coase, Ronald H. (1975), 'Economists and Public Policy', in *Large Corporations in a Changing Society*, ed. J. Fred Weston, New York University Press, New York. Reprinted in Coase's *Essays on Economics and Economists*, University of Chicago Press, Chicago: 47–63. Reprinted in D. B. Klein (ed.), *What Do Economists Contribute?*, Macmillan, London, and New York University Press, New York, 1999: 33–52.

Gieringer, Dale H. (1985), 'The Safety and Efficacy of New Drug Approval', *Cato Journal* 5(1): 177–201.

Hayek, Friedrich A. (1960), *The Constitution of Liberty*, University of Chicago Press, Chicago.

Healy, Elaine M., and Kenneth Kaitin (1999), 'The European Agency for the Evaluation of Medicinal Product's Centralized Procedure for Product Approval: Current Status', *Drug Information Journal* 33: 969–78.

Higgs, Robert (1995), 'How FDA Is Causing a Technological Exodus: A Comparative Analysis of Medical Device Regulation – United States, Europe, Canada, and Japan', Competitive Enterprise Institute, Washington, DC, March.

Kaitin, Kenneth I., and Jeffrey S. Brown (1995), 'AA Drug Lag Update', *Drug Information Journal* 29: 361–73.

Mises, Ludwig von (1940), 'My Contributions to Economic Theory', address, in *Planning for Freedom*, fourth ed., Libertarian Press, South Holland, Illinois, 1980: 224–33.

Peltzman, Sam (1973), 'The Benefits and Costs of New Drug Regulation', *Regulating New Drugs*, ed. Richard L. Landau,

University of Chicago Press, Chicago: 114–211.

Stigler, George J. (1982), *The Economist as Preacher and Other Essays*, University of Chicago Press, Chicago.

Tabarrok, Alexander (2000), 'Assessing the FDA via the Anomaly of Off-Label Drug Prescribing', *The Independent Review* 5, #1: 25–53.

ABOUT THE IEA

The Institute is a research and educational charity (No. CC 235 351), limited by guarantee. Its mission is to improve understanding of the fundamental institutions of a free society with particular reference to the role of markets in solving economic and social problems.

The IEA achieves its mission by:

- a high quality publishing programme
- conferences, seminars, lectures and other events
- outreach to school and college students
- brokering media introductions and appearances

The IEA, which was established in 1955 by the late Sir Antony Fisher, is an educational charity, not a political organisation. It is independent of any political party or group and does not carry on activities intended to affect support for any political party or candidate in any election or referendum, or at any other time. It is financed by sales of publications, conference fees and voluntary donations.

In addition to its main series of publications the IEA also publishes a quarterly journal, *Economic Affairs*, and has two specialist programmes – Environment and Technology, and Education.

The IEA is aided in its work by a distinguished international Academic Advisory Council and an eminent panel of Honorary Fellows. Together with other academics, they review prospective IEA publications, their comments being passed on anonymously to authors. All IEA papers are therefore subject to the same rigorous independent refereeing process as used by leading academic journals.

IEA publications enjoy widespread classroom use and course adoptions in schools and universities. They are also sold throughout the world and often translated/reprinted.

Since 1974 the IEA has helped to create a world-wide network of 100 similar institutions in over 70 countries. They are all independent but share the IEA's mission.

Views expressed in the IEA's publications are those of the authors, not those of the Institute (which has no corporate view), its Managing Trustees, Academic Advisory Council members or senior staff.

Members of the Institute's Academic Advisory Council, Honorary Fellows, Trustees and Staff are listed on the following page.

The Institute gratefully acknowledges financial support for its publications programme and other work from a generous benefaction by the late Alec and Beryl Warren.

For information about subscriptions to IEA publications, please contact:

Subscriptions
The Institute of Economic Affairs
2 Lord North Street
London SW1P 3LB

Tel: 020 7799 8900
Fax: 020 7799 2137
Website: www.iea.org.uk/books/subscribe.htm

Other papers recently published by the IEA include:

WHO, What and Why?

Transnational Government, Legitimacy and the World Health Organization
Roger Scruton
Occasional Paper 113
ISBN 0 255 36487 3

The World Turned Rightside Up

A New Trading Agenda for the Age of Globalisation
John C. Hulsman
Occasional Paper 114
ISBN 0 255 36495 4

The Representation of Business in English Literature

Introduced and edited by Arthur Pollard
Readings 53
ISBN 0 255 36491 1

Anti-Liberalism 2000

The Rise of New Millennium Collectivism
David Henderson
Occasional Paper 115
ISBN 0 255 36497 0

Capitalism, Morality and Markets
Brian Griffiths, Robert A. Sirico, Norman Barry and Frank Field
Readings 54
ISBN 0 255 36496 2

A Conversation with Harris and Seldon
Ralph Harris and Arthur Seldon
Occasional Paper 116
ISBN 0 255 36498 9

Malaria and the DDT Story
Richard Tren & Roger Bate
Occasional Paper 117
ISBN 0 255 36499 7

To order copies of currently available IEA papers, or to enquire about availability, please contact:

Lavis Marketing
73 Lime Walk
Oxford OX3 7AD

Tel: 01865 767575
Fax: 01865 750079
Email: orders@lavismarketing.co.uk